UNDERSTANDING SCIENCE & NATURE

Animal Behavior

TIME-LIFE
ALEXANDRIA, VIRGINIA

C O N T E N T S

3 Mating and Parenting 88

4 Animal Social Behavior 124

1
Finding Food

Animals' lives are shaped by basic needs. They need shelter to live in. They need to reproduce themselves by giving birth. They need to protect themselves from their enemies. And they need to find food.

Unlike humans, animals cannot grow their own vegetables or herd cattle: They must hunt for their dinner. This quest for food has caused animals to develop remarkable senses and abilities. A barn owl, for instance, can catch a mouse in complete darkness, using only its ears to pinpoint the faint rustling of leaves. Winding swiftly

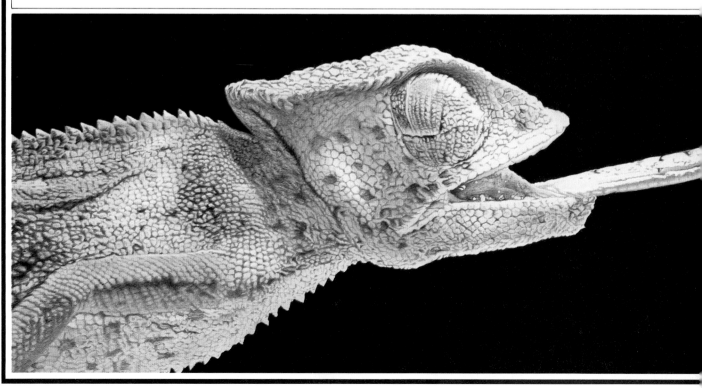

across the ground, a snake can sense the path of its prey with its flickering tongue. Some animals, such as chimpanzees, have learned to make food-finding tools out of sticks or leaves. Others live together in a cooperative arrangement known as symbiosis, in which each animal helps the other. The methods that animals use to seek out their meals are almost as numerous as the animals themselves.

These diverse adaptations have allowed animals to feed and survive in almost every nook and cranny of the Earth, from the bird-filled for-

ests of the Amazon to the krill-rich seas of the Antarctic. This chapter is an examination of the extraordinary bodies, behavior, and senses of a number of animals, both big and small, as they seek out their food.

Unhampered by darkness, a barn owl carries off its prey *(above)*. Animals such as the owl and the chameleon, shown below snagging a moth, have developed keen reflexes to snare their fast-moving food.

How Does a Paramecium Feed Itself?

Paramecia are among the smallest, simplest animals on Earth. Found wherever there is fresh water, the slipper-shaped creatures are usually too tiny to be seen with the naked eye. Despite their simplicity, paramecia search out and gobble down food with as much energy as their bigger and better-known cousins in the animal world.

A paramecium's body consists of a single cell covered by thousands of short, hairlike strands called cilia. The cilia beat rhythmically to move the minute animal and to pull food, such as other one-celled animals and tiny plants, toward its body. Although a paramecium doesn't have eyes or a nose, it can sense chemicals around it, including the chemicals given off by food. These substances trigger electrical impulses in the creature's body, making the cilia beat in the direction of the prey. The paramecium moves forward until the chemical "taste" weakens. Then it turns, moves forward again, and repeats the action so that it seems to circle the food in a decreasing spiral, finally reaching the goal *(right)*.

Once the paramecium finds its prey, its cilia create a current and sweep the food into its oral groove. Often the little animal will reject particles that are not nutritious, and like creatures much larger, it will prefer some foods to others.

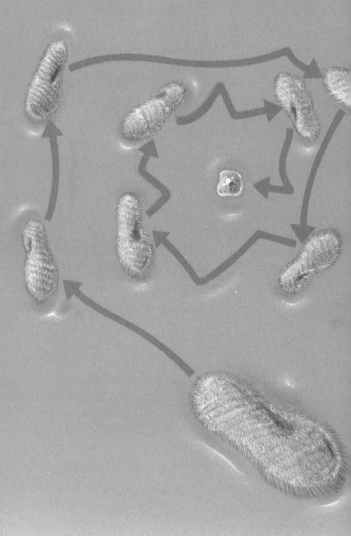

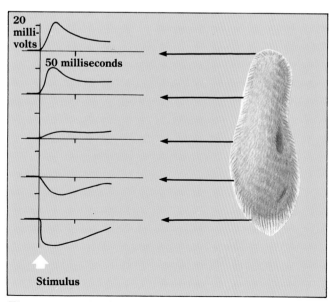

The paramecium reacts in different ways to electrical stimulation of its body. For instance, if the front is stimulated, the cilia will beat backward and the animal will turn.

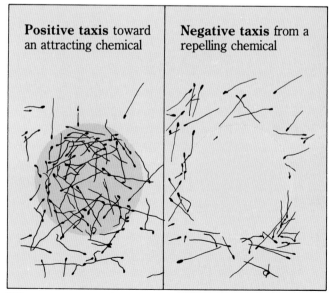

Positive taxis toward an attracting chemical

Negative taxis from a repelling chemical

When a paramecium turns and moves toward the source of a stimulus, that movement is called positive taxis. Movement away from a stimulus is negative taxis.

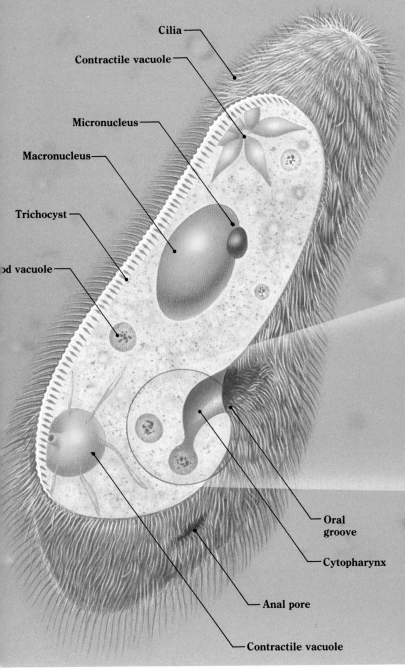

Cilia

Contractile vacuole

Micronucleus

Macronucleus

Trichocyst

[Fo]od vacuole

Oral groove

Cytopharynx

Anal pore

Contractile vacuole

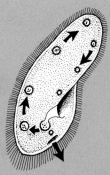

After food enters a paramecium, a bubble, or vacuole, forms around it. Chemicals called enzymes digest the food as the vacuole travels through the body. Waste departs by the anal pore.

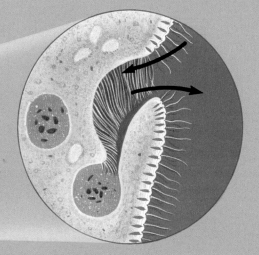

A paramecium feeds on tiny organisms, such as bacteria, that live in the water. Inside its oral groove *(above)*, rippling, hairlike cilia act as a sieve, trapping solid matter drawn in with the water. This matter then collects in a food vacuole, which balloons out to hold it. When the food has broken down into even smaller particles, it is stored in the animal's body. Other vacuoles collect extra water and spew it out of the cell.

What eats the paramecium?

Paramecia belong to a large group of one-celled animals called protozoans. Their relatives are not always friendly; in fact, one kind of protozoan, called didinium, will attack and eat the larger paramecium. When a didinium nears a paramecium, it chases it around and around in a circle until the two collide. Then it shoots two harpoonlike structures out of a long tube near its mouth, paralyzing the paramecium's cilia. The didinium withdraws its harpoons and begins to swallow the paramecium, although the prey is larger than its captor. In less than two minutes, a didinium can entirely swallow a paramecium.

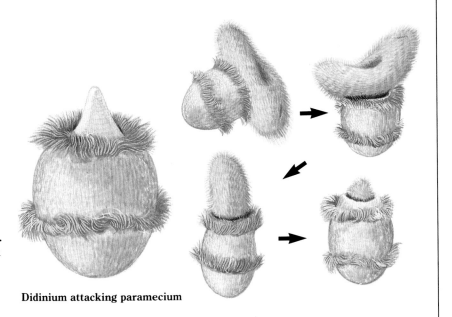

Didinium attacking paramecium

How Do Flies Eat?

The housefly, a familiar but unwelcome visitor to households around the world, has lived successfully among people for thousands of years. This is due in part to the insect's well-developed senses of smell and taste, which enable it to find food that humans have left out.

Houseflies smell with their antennae. Small holes in the two appendages contain tiny sensory hairs that can detect odors—such as the ripe smell of the rotting meat and vegetables that the fly prefers. Once the fly discovers the food, it must walk on it because its taste buds are located in sensory hairs on its feet and on the lip at the tip of its proboscis, a funnel-like mouth. If the food is edible, the fly lowers its proboscis to eat.

The fly uses the sensory hairs on its feet to find out if a piece of food is edible. Then it uncoils its proboscis and checks the morsel again with the hairs on its lip before it eats.

Sensory pits cover a housefly's antennae and give the insect its sense of smell. Female flies usually have more pits than males.

When it picks up the scent of food in the air, a fly will first prick up its antennae to find the source of the odor. As it flies, it will continue to check the direction of the smell.

Sensory hairs on a fly's lip, magnified here by an electron microscope, are connected to nerves that perceive taste.

Like its lip, each of a fly's six feet is covered with tiny hairs that pick up the taste of food.

How Do Mosquitoes Locate Blood?

Hapless humans slapping at mosquitoes whining near their ears often wonder how the tiny insects find them. But to a mosquito, a warm-blooded human stands out from its surroundings.

Only female mosquitoes drink blood. They find their prey by following light, heat, and scent. Mosquitoes have well-developed eyesight; at night, they can see lighted houses from far away. When they are close to prey, sensory organs in their antennae detect odors given off by sweat, hormones, amino acids, and a mixture of oily substances on a person's skin. The insects can also sense carbon dioxide gas and warm moist air released when an animal exhales.

Drawn by the smells and by body heat, a female mosquito approaches a victim. It settles on the skin, probes the skin with its proboscis (a tubelike mouth), and begins to suck up blood.

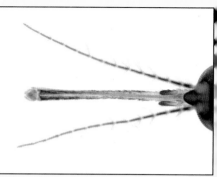

Proboscis and antennae

What attracts mosquitoes?

To find out which factors really attract mosquitoes, scientists set up an experiment in a wind tunnel. Inside the tunnel were three funnels. The one on the left released warm, moist air; the one in the middle released cool, moist air; and the one on the right released hot, dry air. Then the scientists introduced hundreds of tropical mosquitoes, adding carbon dioxide to the air to stimulate the insects. The researchers found that most insects collected near the funnel emitting warm, moist air. This showed that it is a combination of factors that draws mosquitoes, not heat or moisture alone.

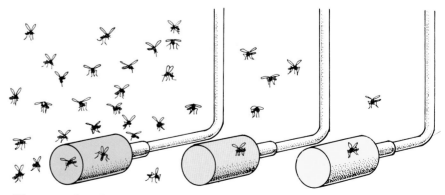

Warm, moist air attracted about 92% of the insects.

Moist air only brought in 5% of the insects.

Warm air attracted just 3% of the mosquitoes.

On entering a house, a mosquito will fly about at random until it senses a current of warm, moist air and carbon dioxide. As soon as it picks up this current, it turns and flies toward the source of the vapors. Constantly changing direction, the mosquito tracks down the spot where the emission of carbon dioxide is strongest.

How mosquitoes suck blood

When a female mosquito has landed on a victim, it places the lip on the tip of its proboscis on the victim's skin. Then it pierces the surface with the sharp, needlelike lancets in its upper and lower mandibles, or mouth parts. The lip itself does not pierce the skin but rests just behind the lancets, bending back into the shape of a bow to stabilize and support them. It is possible to see the blood flow from the victim to the mosquito while it is sucking.

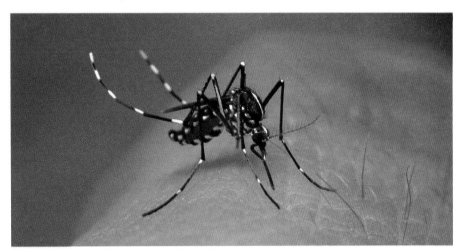

An *Aedes albopictus* mosquito makes a meal.

How Do Ants Use Aphids?

Certain types of ants and aphids enjoy a relationship known as symbiosis, in which different species help each other to survive. Aphids—tiny, slow-moving insects that live on plants—feed on nectar, which they suck out of plant stems with their long, pointed mouths. As they digest the nectar, it is turned into a sugary substance called honeydew, which they then release through specialized organs called cornicles. Honeydew is a favorite food of dairying ants, which eat as much of it as the aphids can produce. By keeping their own private "herd" of aphids, ants have a readily available food supply.

To protect their supply of honeydew, ants take good care of their aphids. For example, they will move the aphids to a place where they can find enough nectar, and when that feeding area becomes too crowded they will move them to a roomier one. Ants will also attack any insect that tries to eat the aphids, even if the invader is much larger than they are.

Scientists are not sure when or how this remarkable relationship began. But the discovery of fossilized ants and aphids together shows that the two types of insects have been helping each other for at least 30 million years.

Protecting the aphids. The ladybug is a natural enemy of aphids, and when one attacks, the ants will band together to drive it away.

"Milking" an aphid. By stroking an aphid's abdomen with its antennae, an ant induces the smaller insect to release a droplet of honeydew, which the ant drinks from the aphid's cornicle.

A brown ant milks a gall aphid. Gall aphids lay their eggs inside the branches of trees, causing the trees to form round growths called galls—one of which is visible above—around the eggs.

Moving to a new home. When aphids overcrowd their feeding area, ants will pick them up in their mouths and carry them to a location with more food.

Why Do Snakes Flick Out Their Tongues?

Although snakes have sensitive noses, they breathe very slowly and cannot sniff the air quickly enough to follow the scent of their prey. They have developed an additional organ, called Jacobson's organ, for detecting odors.

Because Jacobson's organ is deep inside the mouth, a snake must extend its tongue to pick up odors that its prey has left in the air and on the ground. The tongue then withdraws and brings these scents back to Jacobson's organ. Since snakes dart their tongues in and out rapidly, they quickly zero in on and follow the smell of even the fastest animals.

How a snake uses its tongue

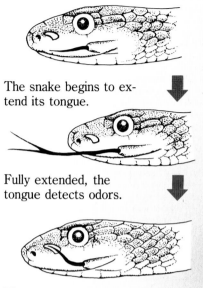

The snake begins to extend its tongue.

Fully extended, the tongue detects odors.

The snake pulls back its tongue, taking the odors to Jacobson's organ.

Named after L. L. Jacobson, the nineteenth-century Danish scientist who discovered it, Jacobson's organ consists of two hollows in the roof of a snake's mouth. Each is lined with chemical receptors that can detect very faint odors.

Detecting odors

All animals leave traces of themselves as they move, in the gases they exhale and in their sweat, as well as in the bits of skin and hair they leave on the ground. In tracking an animal, a snake probes for gases by darting its tongue in the air and then touches its tongue to the ground to detect particles. These gases and particles dissolve into the snake's tongue, which carries them to Jacobson's organ.

14

Reptiles with Jacobson's organ

Grass snake

Komodo dragon

Favorite prey

Wondering how snakes identify the smell of their natural prey, scientists took newborn snakes and exposed them to the scents of various animals. The snakes darted their tongues most often when they scented their normal prey—even though they had never smelled any animal before. For example, the northern banded water snake had the strongest response to the smell of frogs, which are the staple of its diet, while queen snakes darted their tongues the fastest for the smell of crayfish, their usual food. This implies that every snake is born with a sensitivity to the smell of certain animals. The graphs at right show the tongue extensions per minute of two types of snakes exposed to the smells of worms, frogs, fish, mice, insects, and crayfish.

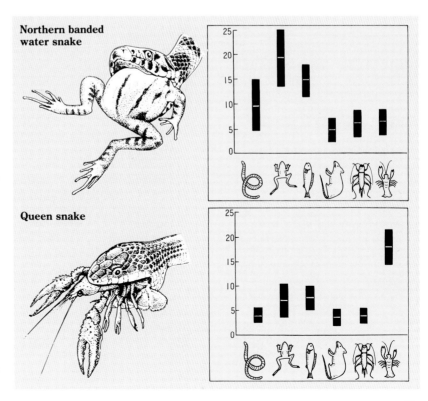

Northern banded water snake

Queen snake

Why Do Woodpeckers Peck at Trees?

Woodpeckers earn their name because of their persistent search for food. Using their hard, pointed beaks, these birds chip away tree bark to expose both adult insects, which live in cracks and crevices in the bark, and larval insects called grubs, which burrow into the wood of the trees. Aiding woodpeckers in their search for insects are their long, whiplike tongues, which they use to probe hard-to-reach places.

Woodpeckers are well suited for digging into wood. Their strong head and neck muscles allow them to hammer at the ferocious rate of 20 pecks per second, while special cushioning in their heads absorbs the shocks of repeated strikes. Furthermore, their unusually strong claws and tails give them a firm grip even on vertical tree trunks.

A woodpecker's beak is chisel shaped, extremely hard, and very efficient for chipping away wood. Inside the bird's head, between its beak and skull, lies a layer of spongy material that acts as a natural shock absorber.

Each foot has two claws pointed forward, two backward.

Woodpeckers' bodies are specially adapted so that they can hold onto trees while pecking.

Thick, hard tail feathers help woodpeckers balance.

Making a gold bed

In addition to eating insects, some woodpeckers also eat nuts. The North American acorn woodpecker *(right),* for instance, will store up to 50,000 acorns in trees, utility poles, and other wooden structures. The nuts are tightly wedged into holes, and the acorn woodpecker will attack and drive away any interlopers hoping to steal from the vast hoard.

Other birds, such as the great spotted woodpecker, use an inventive technique known as wedge driving to crack nuts open. When the woodpecker has found a nut to eat, it will stick it between forking branches of a tree or in a large crack in the tree's bark. When no wedge is available, the bird will peck one out of the tree itself. With the nut securely fastened, the woodpecker pecks the shell open and eats the meat. Woodpeckers will use the same wedge, called a gold bed, for an entire season, leaving behind a large pile of cracked shells.

The woodpecker's tongue

Supporting a woodpecker's tongue is the hyoid, a long structure of bone and elastic tissue. Anchored near the upper beak, it wraps around the skull and is extremely flexible, allowing a woodpecker to stick its tongue into very tight spaces.

Hyoid

Tongue

Using its long tongue, a woodpecker locates a grub. To help woodpeckers hold onto their prey once they have found it, their tongues are coated with a sticky, mucuslike substance. The tongues of many woodpeckers also have sharp points and barbs, which help them pull insects out of tight holes and cracks.

17

How Does a Platypus Find Food?

The duckbilled platypus, a mammal native to the lakes and rivers of Australia, can find food underwater with its eyes, ears, and nose shut tight. It manages this feat because its bill has special cells *(below)* that can sense the electric fields the prey generates.

The platypus feeds mainly on shrimp and other crustaceans. To find these creatures, it dives underwater and scans the bottom until it picks up the electric signals that scientists believe these animals give off. When the platypus has found such a signal, it roots around in the mud until its bill touches the signal's source. Then it snaps up its meal.

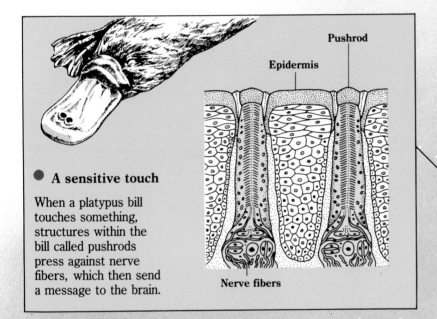

Pushrod

Epidermis

● **A sensitive touch**

When a platypus bill touches something, structures within the bill called pushrods press against nerve fibers, which then send a message to the brain.

Nerve fibers

How a platypus lives

Platypuses hunt for food at night and spend their days in tunnels they dig near lakes and rivers. To guard against predators, they often plug the ends of their tunnels with dirt. Unlike almost all other mammals, female platypuses lay eggs, which they incubate in nests lined with wet leaves. When the eggs hatch, the young feed off the mother's milk *(far right)*.

Instead of teeth, adult platypuses have "grinding pads," flat plates of bone that extend into the mouth and are well suited for grinding food.

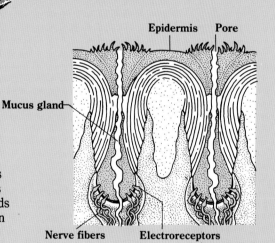

Epidermis   Pore

Mucus gland

Nerve fibers   Electroreceptors

● **Sensing electricity**

The left side of a platypus bill contains tiny pores, each one leading to nerves that detect electric fields. Mucus glands keep the pores and nerves moist when the platypus is out of the water.

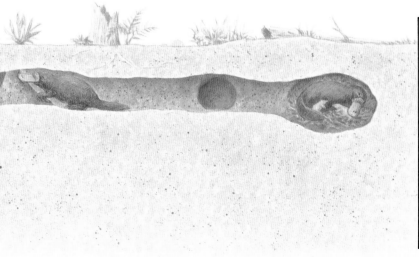

A platypus nurses her young.

Why Do Catfish Have Whiskers?

Catfish and loach, two widespread species of primarily freshwater fish, cannot rely on their eyes as they hunt for food along dark, muddy river bottoms. Therefore, these fish have evolved specialized, whiskerlike organs called barbels that enable them to sift through mud and sand in order to find the insects and fish that they eat.

Barbels are long appendages on the fish's upper and lower lips that contain taste buds similar to those found in the tongues of most animals. By simply swimming through the water with its barbels extended, or brushing its barbels across a riverbed, a fish can recognize the taste of the animals near it. When its barbels detect a tasty animal, the fish swallows it.

Anatomy of a loach barbel

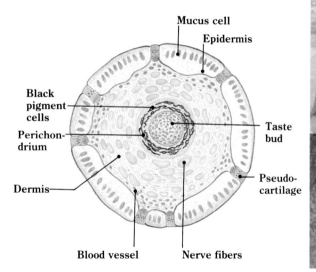

- Mucus cell
- Epidermis
- Black pigment cells
- Perichondrium
- Taste bud
- Dermis
- Pseudo-cartilage
- Blood vessel
- Nerve fibers

Loach hunt for insect larvae *(below)* by sticking their barbels in the mud and moving their heads back and forth.

Barbels for every environment

Different types of fish have evolved different types of barbels to suit their environments. For instance, loaches that live in muddy places such as rice fields have long, supple barbels that they drag through the soft mud in search of food. Others, such as the spiny loach, have shorter, stiffer barbels for probing sandy or gravelly riverbeds. The barbels of still others have been almost completely replaced by mouths shaped like suction cups with which they pull algae off rocks. These different types of barbels are illustrated at right.

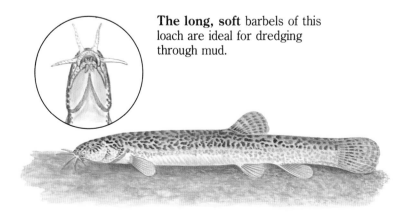

The long, soft barbels of this loach are ideal for dredging through mud.

Bullhead catfish *(above)* move their barbels vigorously through sand and gravel in search of food.

A channel catfish *(right)* swims with its barbels sticking straight out, waiting for a small fish to brush against them.

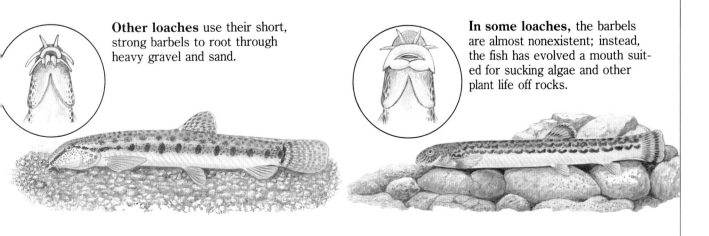

Other loaches use their short, strong barbels to root through heavy gravel and sand.

In some loaches, the barbels are almost nonexistent; instead, the fish has evolved a mouth suited for sucking algae and other plant life off rocks.

How Do These Creatures Help Each Other?

Finding food in the animal kingdom is not always a matter of kill or be killed. Some creatures have learned to cooperate in the mutually helpful relationship called symbiosis.

Such an arrangement can be found in the Bahamas among sea anemones, shrimp, and fish. The brightly colored cleaner shrimp set up "feeding stations" among the tentacles of large, poisonous sea anemones. Fish swim up to the shrimp, which then eat parasites attached to the fish's body. The sea anemones protect the shrimp from predators and sometimes grab and eat the fish.

] **A fish gets as close** as it dares to a cleaner shrimp on the tentacles of a sea anemone.

▶**Having come too close** to the anemone's tentacles, a fish is stung to death.

Other symbiotic cleaners

Cleaning symbiosis can be seen throughout the marine world. Various kinds of shrimp and fish specialize in cleaning other sea creatures. This provides food for the cleaners and comfort for the animal being cleaned.

Cleaners usually have bright patterns, probably because this makes them noticeable. The service they provide is so popular that a line of fish may form by the feeding station, each one waiting to be cleaned.

A cleaner shrimp enters the mouth of a fish to eat tiny animals, bacteria, or fungi caught in the fish's teeth.

A shrimp cleans a leopard moray's mouth and does so without any danger of being eaten.

2 A fish tips to one side to entice a shrimp to remove its parasites. In response, the shrimp swims over.

3 Clinging to the fish's body, a cleaner shrimp eats tiny crustaceans around its eye.

Why Do Remoras Stick to Sharks?

Sometimes one animal gets more out of a symbiotic relationship than the other. Such is the case with the remora.

A remora is an odd fish that hitches rides on sharks and other sea creatures using a sucker on top of its head. It benefits in several ways from its free ride. For one thing, it saves energy when it is carried by the shark; even when it detaches from the larger animal it is carried along in the bow wave created by the moving shark. Furthermore, the remora has easy access to food, snacking on little crustaceans attached to its host's body or on scraps that drop from the shark's mouth. Predators are also unlikely to attack the remoras when they are accompanied by a shark.

Sharks gain from the arrangement, too, when remoras eat the parasites that infest them. Nevertheless, the remoras seem to have the best end of the bargain.

■ **How remoras collect parasites**

A remora's bottom jaw sticks out far beyond its top jaw. This is a convenient adaptation for collecting and eating the parasites scraped off a shark's body.

When a remora moves forward along a shark's body, its upper jaw acts like a spatula to scrape parasites from the shark's skin. The crustaceans then fall into the remora's lower jaw.

▲ **The remora's oval sucker,** formed from a rippled bone, evolved from a fin on top of its body. About three weeks after a remora hatches, its sucker is completely formed, and the remora is able to attach itself to other fish.

● **Other hosts for remoras**

Remoras also cling to rays, whales, sea turtles—and even deep-sea divers.

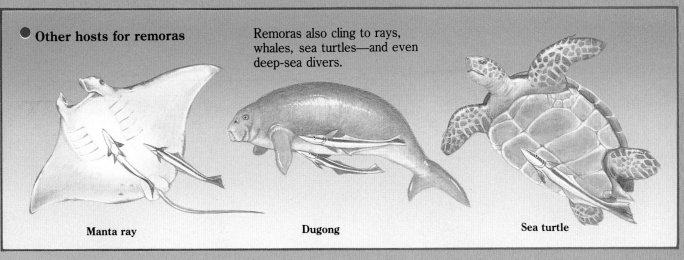

Manta ray   Dugong   Sea turtle

How Do Spiders Capture Their Prey?

Among the more than 32,000 known species of spiders there are many ingenious ways of capturing prey. For instance, all spiders spin silk from special organs in their bodies called spinnerets. The strongest of natural fibers, spider silk can be dry or sticky, and many spiders use their silk to build webs to capture the insects that they eat. Some spiders spin webs with just a few strands; others use their silk only for nest building, while some spin a tiny web that they throw over their prey like a net.

Some spiders do not spin webs. Instead, they ambush or chase their prey, or even lure it into a trap. Each species has developed its own way of capturing prey, a strategy perfectly suited to its environment.

Dangling above the ground, the spectacled spider holds a small, stretchy web taut with four of its legs, then suddenly spreads it over its prey.

Hidden within outspread petals, a shamrock spider *(left)* lies motionless, waiting for insects to visit the bloom. When a bee arrives *(right)*, the spider seizes it.

From a silk-lined burrow with a hinged door *(below)*, a trapdoor spider darts out to catch a sow bug *(right)*.

Hanging from its simple web, the Australian honeycomb spider dangles a gob of sticky, scented silk on a line *(far left)*. When a moth lured by the scent gets stuck to the ball *(left)*, the spider hauls it up and eats it.

The spitting spider lurks in dark corners, shooting a sticky liquid out of its mouth and over its prey as it comes within range. This substance hardens and traps the victim.

A wolf spider holds a baby mouse it has caught without using a web or snare. This hunting spider prowls on the ground, spotting prey as much as 10 inches away, then dashing to catch it and paralyzing it with a bite.

The six-starred fishing spider clings to a riverbank with its back legs and taps the surface of the water with its front legs. Fooled by this imitation of an insect, fish come to the surface, where the spider grabs them.

How Do Spiders Sense Prey in a Web?

Most spiders have poor eyesight and rely instead on an acute sense of touch to find out what is going on around them. Because a spider's legs pick up the slightest vibration, a spider waiting at the edge of its web can detect the movements of its victims as they struggle to escape the web's sticky strands.

The kinds of spiders that spin webs to catch prey usually wait at the hub, or center, of the web or hide in leaves at the web's edge. A spider that hides some distance away extends a communication cord from the web to its hiding place. By keeping its feet on the com-

munication cord, it is aware the moment a victim becomes trapped. If a falling leaf lands in the web, the spider will not go and investigate because it can distinguish between the movements of a leaf and those of its prey.

A victim's vibrations

In an experiment to see how spiders identify prey, a scientist made a tuning fork vibrate at the frequency of an insect's beating wings and touched it to a garden spider's web. The spider reacted exactly as if it had caught real prey. Tested at other frequencies, the spider ran away or stayed still.

A tuning fork *(above)* vibrating at insect wing frequency touches a spider's web. The spider, mistaking the tuning fork for prey, tries to wrap it in silk *(left)*.

Grasping a strand of the web with each clawed foot *(above)*, a spider feels vibrations from other parts of the web. The vibrations reach the spider through tiny hairs bristling on its legs. In fact, the different vibrations reaching each of its eight legs tell the spider exactly where in the web its victim is caught.

● **Alarm system**

▼ **The common garden spider** runs a communication cord from its web to a nearby hideaway, shown at right, where it waits.

▶ **The urocteid spider** spins a dense, flat web and uses the spokes, or radials, as communication cords.

Spiders grip strands of their webs with three claws at the tip of each leg, here magnified 80 times. The bent claw is used to draw new silk from the spinnerets.

A moth stuck in a web tries to free itself by beating its wings. Feeling strands of the web vibrate, the spider hurries toward the trapped creature. The spider will paralyze the moth with a venomous bite, then dine by sucking out its juices.

29

What Is Mimicry?

As its prey approaches, the mantis stays so still that the butterfly takes it for a real orchid blossom.

The mantis strikes out with its forelegs to catch the unsuspecting butterfly. Saw-toothed edges on the mantis's forelegs help it hold its prey.

Found only in the Malayan jungle, the flower mantis is a rare insect shaped and colored much like a pink orchid blossom. This flower impersonation attracts other insects, which the mantis then captures and eats.

A number of animals use this kind of camouflage, called mimicry. Camouflage that helps an animal attack and capture prey is aggressive mimicry. Mimicry also gives protection from natural enemies. As an enemy approaches, a mantis will not run but will stay where it is, and its enemy takes it to be the flower or leaf it resembles, not something to eat.

More mantis mimics

Hugging the bark of a lichen-covered tree, a grizzled mantis can hardly be seen.

Color, shape, and movement help the dead-leaf mantis fool its enemies; it sways gently, like a dry leaf stirring in the breeze.

A lifetime of camouflage

The young flower mantis resembles the assassin bug, which has a painful bite. This mimicry saves the youngster from predators.

As it gets older, the mantis resembles an orchid and can hide in plain sight.

As an adult, the flower mantis changes into a more ordinary looking green mantis.

How Do Chameleons Hunt?

Camouflaged, a chameleon's color now matches a sunny bush.

The chameleon, a lizard native to Europe, Africa, and Asia, is best known for its ability to change color, and this camouflage helps it avoid the notice of its enemies and its prey. But it has three other traits it also uses in hunting: its long, sticky tongue, swiveling eyes, and feet that grip like hands. Hunting by day in its tropical forest home, the chameleon waits motionless on a branch, or slowly stalks, until an insect is within tongue range. Then the tongue, half as long as the chameleon's body and carried compressed in its mouth, shoots out to seize the prey and carry it to the waiting jaws.

Why a chameleon changes color

Although it is said that a chameleon changes its body color so as to blend in with its surroundings, this is not strictly true. A chameleon changes its body color in response to changes in the temperature and brightness around it. Its color will darken in a dim, cool environment and become lighter in a brighter, warmer one. If a chameleon that is in a bright, warm place is partly covered by a thick, cool cloth, the part of its body under the cloth will darken. Chameleons will also become lighter if startled or excited. Such mood-related color changes mean a chameleon does not always match its environment.

1 A frond droops over a basking chameleon.

2 Skin warmed by the frond becomes lighter.

Retracted inside the mouth, the chameleon's tongue is thick and pointed, compressed like a pushed-up sleeve. At its tip, special glands maintain the tongue's moisture with a very sticky secretion.

Choosing a target, the chameleon uses neck, jaw, and tongue muscles to shoot its tongue out so that its tip hits the insect. With the prey stuck fast, the tongue retracts *(below)*—all in a twentieth of a second.

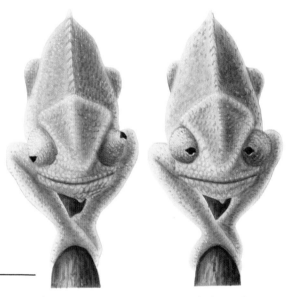

A chameleon's eyes move independently in all directions *(above, left)*, but when the animal takes aim at a victim, both eyes swivel forward to watch the target *(above, right)*. Seen head-on by its prey, the slender reptile looks small and harmless, until it is too late to flee.

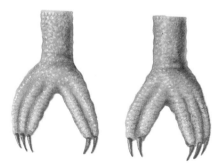

On the chameleon's feet, two toes are set opposite three more toes, giving the animal a solid grip. Even its tail is used to steady the chameleon on its perch.

33

How Do Rattlesnakes Track Their Prey?

To find their prey, rattlesnakes first use their keen sense of smell *(page 14)* to locate a path commonly used by the animal. Then they simply wait for their meal to come along. When an animal approaches, the rattler detects it through the vibrations the animal makes as it walks. As the prey gets closer, the snake uses both its eyes and a pair of special heat-sensing devices called pit organs to home in on it. Once the animal comes within reach, the snake strikes and bites, injecting its prey with a lethal dose of venom.

① **Waiting.** Having identified a fallen log as a path commonly used by mice, a rattlesnake lies in wait. As a mouse walks down the log, the snake senses the vibrations.

② **Sensing.** As the mouse moves closer, the snake makes use of both its eyes and its pit organs to target its victim.

A rattlesnake's range

The range of a snake's pit organs is shorter than that of its eyes. Because the pit organs are closer together than the eyes, their range is also narrower.

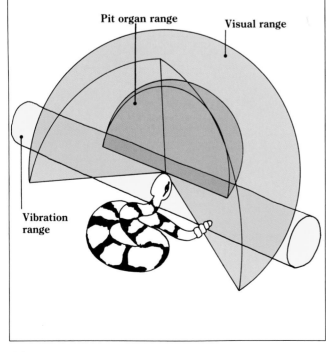

Pit organ range

Visual range

Vibration range

Heat sensors

Just as eyes contain cells that detect light, a rattlesnake's pit organs contain cells that detect heat. Located in the two hollows between the eyes and nostrils, these organs are so sensitive they can distinguish between two objects that differ in temperature by only five-thousandths of a degree Fahrenheit. With these sensors, snakes can hunt even in the dark.

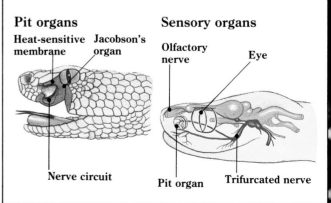

Pit organs

Heat-sensitive membrane   Jacobson's organ

Nerve circuit

Sensory organs

Olfactory nerve

Eye

Pit organ   Trifurcated nerve

▼ **What pit organs "see."** Taken with heat-sensitive film, this photograph of a mouse is similar to what a rattlesnake senses with its pit organs. The warmest areas appear red, the coolest blue.

③ **Striking.** With the mouse in its sights, the snake strikes. Once bitten, the mouse will stumble off for a short distance before dying.

④ **Eating the prey.** After the mouse dies, the rattlesnake tracks its scent to the place where it collapsed. Since snakes have no teeth—aside from their fangs—they must swallow their food whole. Their jaws are specially adapted to spread wide so they can swallow very large animals. In the picture at left, a rattlesnake begins to swallow a mouse it has just killed.

How Does the Green Heron Catch Fish?

The heron, a subfamily of bird that lives on every continent except Antarctica, feeds mainly on fish in shallow lakes and rivers. While most heron catch their fish by hiding among rocks at the water's edge and snatching the first fish that swims by, one type, the green heron, uses bait to lure fish into its grasp. The diagrams below illustrate how the green heron—which is often more blue than green—uses lures to capture its prey.

The green heron uses odds and ends as bait, since fish are attracted more to the lure's motion on the surface of the water than to its composition. Some commonly used objects are fallen leaves, earthworms, and bits of plastic. Observers have even reported that when no suitable lures are available, the birds will break off the end of a twig and use it for bait. Only the green heron uses lures; all other species of heron do not.

Waiting. Using a fallen leaf as a lure, a green heron stands on a rock and waits for fish to pass near.

Lures used by the green heron

Leaf

Nut

Insect

Feather

Broken twig

Setting the trap. As fish swim by, the heron drops the bait into the water. Lured by the splash, the fish move closer.

Snatching the prey. Swiftly, the heron grabs the closest fish. The bird then tilts its head upward, turns the fish around, and swallows its meal headfirst.

Holding a lure in its beak, a green heron stands in shallow water waiting for fish.

37

How Do Barn Owls Hunt in the Dark?

Midnight snack. A barn owl returns to its nest with a mouse.

The barn owl, which hunts at night and often in total darkness, finds and catches its prey by sound alone. Its specially developed ears enable it to track the source of any sound it hears with pinpoint accuracy.

Species of owls that hunt during daylight have large eyes and very sharp eyesight. Owls that hunt in dim light or darkness have eyes sensitive to the dimmest light, as well as very acute hearing. But only the barn owl hunts by sound alone. And while some other land animals also track prey by sound only, the barn owl has the most highly developed hearing. Barn owls hear every faint sound, from a mouse's step to a leaf's fall; what is more important, their specialized ears tell them precisely where a sound comes from.

The barn owl's feathered face

On the barn owl's saucer-shaped face, a layer of soft, fine feathers protects and conceals its ears, which are located on the front of the face, beside the large eyes.

The barn owl's specialized ears

Behind the outer feathers are the barn owl's two ear troughs, formed of hard feathers that reflect sounds to the inner ears. The right ear tilts upward and the left tilts down, and the left earhole (behind a flap of feathered skin) is slightly higher than the right.

Targeting prey

Plummeting through the night air, a barn owl tracks a squirrel above it and a mouse below. Because of its tilted ear troughs *(below, left)*, the owl hears the squirrel's sounds better in its right ear and the mouse's better in its left. When an owl turns toward a sound's source, it is said to use sound orientation.

Swooping to seize the mouse, the owl turns its talons for a perfect catch. The owl makes this adjustment even in the dark, since it can tell by listening which way the mouse is headed.

Catching moving prey

A barn owl flying in pursuit of a mouse *(right)* relies on the noises the mouse makes as it tries to escape. The owl needs to know not only whether it is flying to the left or right of its prey, but how high it is above it. As it flies, the owl always keeps its face turned toward the source of the sounds. In this way, it continually hears the mouse's sounds and corrects its flight path so that it reaches the ground and the mouse's exact location at the same instant.

How Do Whales Eat?

All whales are either hunters or grazers, depending on how their mouths are equipped. The toothed whales pursue, attack, and kill their prey; many use sonar to aid them in the hunt. Instead of teeth, the grazers, or baleen whales, have a sievelike array of hairy-edged plates called baleen. A baleen whale fills its mouth with water, then strains the water through the baleen, eating the remaining small plants and animals.

▲ **Humpback whale.** This baleen whale blows masses of bubbles into a school of fish above it. When the fish are caught in a curtain of bubbles, the whale will gulp the entire school in one mouthful.

▲ **Sperm whale.** Armed with huge teeth and specialized lungs, a sperm whale attacks a giant squid at a depth of 3,000 feet.

▼**Killer whale.** Living in stable family groups, killer whales use teamwork to corner and kill prey. They usually eat fish, attacking larger sea animals only when fish are scarce.

◄**Gray whale.** Turned on its side, this baleen whale scrapes the ocean floor, churning up crustaceans and lugworms. It filters mouthfuls of them from the sandy, silty water.

41

How Do Bats Find Prey at Night?

Humans invented sonar, an echolocation system based on sound waves, in the twentieth century. But bats have used a similar system for thousands of years. As they fly, bats emit high-frequency cries, pulses of sound too high-pitched for humans to hear. The way these sounds bounce off nearby objects and return to the bat's ears enables the bat to navigate in the dark.

Warm-blooded and furry, bats are the only mammals that can truly fly. Some eat fruit and some eat fish, but most live on flying insects and feed on the wing, as in the case of the greater horseshoe bat shown on these pages. A large colony of bats can eat as much as 275 tons of insects in a night, helping to hold down populations of mosquitoes and other harmful insects.

Capture. Catching up with the moth, the bat envelops its prey with its scooplike wings and its tail. The bat's speed and accuracy give the moth scant chance of escaping.

Detection. Having found a moth by using echolocation, a greater horseshoe bat emits its cries more often and flies in pursuit, closing in on its fleeing victim.

● **Sonic fishing**

Skimming along over water, a fishing bat uses the echoes of its sonic pulses to spot the ripple caused by a fish just under the surface. Then it captures the fish with the long claws of its webbed feet. Experiments have shown that fishing bats are able to detect the slightest disturbance of water, such as that made when the tip of a fin breaks the surface.

Using echoes from prey

A bat in normal flight emits from 5 to 20 sonic pulses per second. When it finds prey, however, it emits extra signals—perhaps 100 per second —checking its victim's position with each pulse. If the bat gets closer to the prey, such as a moth, the time between a pulse and its echo diminishes. If the distance from the bat to the moth increases, so does the time between pulse and echo. Thus a bat can tell which way the moth is going.

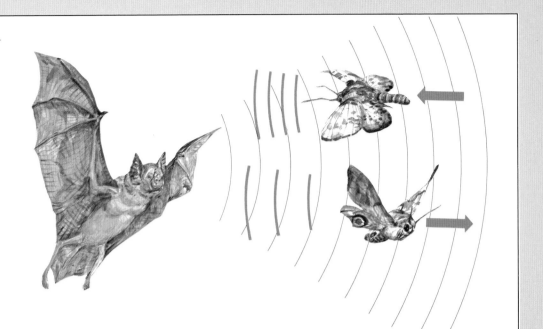

Consumption. The bat catches the moth in its mouth, devouring it at once, and flies on in search of more food. Detection, pursuit, capture, and consumption form one smooth and often-repeated sequence for the bat.

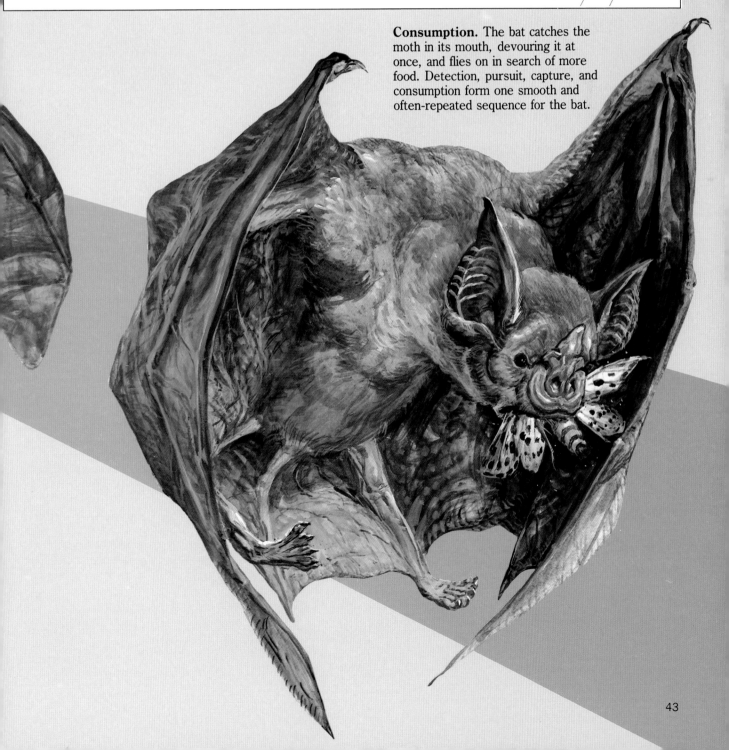

How Does a Wolf Pack Hunt?

The largest members of the dog family, wolves prey on some of the largest members of the deer family. Individuals in their close-knit, highly organized packs are ranked by gender and age. The dominant and strongest male is the leader and outranks all other pack members; generally, older wolves outrank younger ones.

To prey successfully on animals large enough to feed the whole pack, wolves must hunt as teams, with a minimum of conflict. While the older, more experienced wolves lead the hunt and the younger, less experienced ones mainly watch and learn, every member of the pack has a role in the hunt, and all feed on the kill.

How wolves bring down their prey

Wolves usually begin each hunt trotting along with the leader out in front. Catching the scent of prey—here, a moose—the pack stalks in earnest, judging quickly whether it is a likely quarry. A healthy moose will turn to put a large tree at its back and menace the approaching wolves. Knowing from experience that attacking such an animal is a dangerous waste of time and energy, the pack will normally leave it alone. However, a moose that is weak—sick, old, or very young—will try to run from the pack, and that is the one the wolves will hunt. Tireless and persistent in pursuing prey, a wolf pack might travel a few miles or 50 in one expedition; they have been known to cover 125 miles in a day.

The chase. The pack leader starts the chase, but other wolves take turns as the front runner, as in a relay race.

The halt. As the prey tires, the bolder, younger wolves bring it to a halt, biting and snapping at its flanks and muzzle.

The kill. When the moose stops trying to escape, the wolves attack. A kill will feed the pack for three days.

Six snarling wolves slash at a kicking moose. At 1,000 pounds or more, the moose outweighs each wolf by 10; but the wolves outnumber the moose.

The wolf's code of behavior

For a wolf pack, survival depends on working together. A pack that quarrels cannot cooperate on where to go, where to rest, or which animal to hunt, and a pack unable to hunt successfully cannot survive. To help avoid quarrels, wolves have a strict hierarchy, expressed and confirmed by their dominant and submissive behaviors.

Passive submission. A wolf asserts its superiority over another by leaning over it *(below).* The lower-ranking wolf submits by lying on its back with its paws in the air.

A greeting gesture. As the leader approaches, another pack member rolls onto its side at his feet, showing that it does not challenge him.

Active submission. To the pack leader *(above, right),* another male shows active submission; ears and tail down, teeth bared in a grin, he gently licks the leader's muzzle.

45

How Do Chimpanzees Use Tools?

For a long time, people believed that humans were the only animals to use tools. But in the 1960s, scientists found that chimpanzees used sticks, stones, leaves, and other objects to get food and water. Sometimes they pushed sticks into underground honeybee nests to reach the honey. They also used leaves as sponges or turned sticks into levers to open boxes of food.

Researchers around the world have seen other animals pick up objects to help them get at food or probe unfamiliar items. Scientists now define humans as the only animals able to use one tool to craft another from a set pattern.

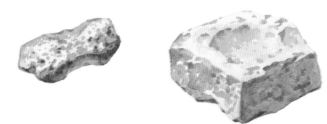

Chimpanzees can use stone tools, such as the one pictured above, for opening nuts.

Cracking nuts. Using two rocks as a hammer and table, a chimp pounds nuts to crack their shells and reach the tender meat.

Handmade tools.
Chimps engage in crude toolmaking, stripping leaves from a twig or peeling off the edges of a wide blade of grass. These tools are usually used for capturing insects, probing new objects, and sometimes for picking teeth.

Gathering water. With a leafy sponge, a chimp can retrieve water from hard-to-reach places like the hollows of a tree.

Collecting termites. A chimp pokes a stick into a termite nest, then eats the clinging insects.

Probing the unfamiliar. A chimp uses a stick to prod a snake, finding out if the reptile poses a danger.

Other animals that use tools

Egyptian vultures hurl rocks to crack thick-shelled ostrich eggs.

Woodpecker finches use cactus thorns to dig bugs out of the bark of trees.

Sea otters smash open clams and other tasty shellfish with rocks.

How Do Sea Anemones Capture Fish?

Although it looks like a colorful flower growing from the ocean floor, a sea anemone is actually a meat-eating animal, trapping its prey in gaudy tentacles. This sea creature attaches itself to the bottom of the sea along tidal zones, where waves might wash fish or crustaceans into its reach. Then the anemone injects the prey, such as a fish, with poison from stinging cells lining the tips of its tentacles. In some anemones, the stinging cells are sticky, trapping the prey as well as poisoning it. Once captured, the fish is gradually drawn into the anemone's spacious mouth and eaten.

Stinging cells line the sea anemone's tentacles and gut.

Poisonous harpoons

Inside each stinging cell, called a nematocyst, is a poisonous spine attached to a coiled filament. When touched by prey, it uncoils and shoots out.

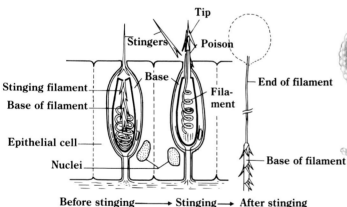

Tip

Stingers — Poison

Stinging filament — Base — End of filament

Base of filament — Fila-ment

Epithelial cell —

Nuclei — — Base of filament

Before stinging ⟶ Stinging ⟶ After stinging

● **The dangerous hydra**

A small relative of the sea anemone, the hydra has a simple tubelike body and a few tentacles surrounding the mouth. Like the anemone, it looks deceptively innocent, for it too contains nematocysts with which to poison prey—larvae, water fleas, and other small animals.

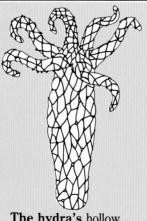

The hydra's hollow body has two cell layers.

2
Animal
Defenses

Every animal must eat something and for a group of hunters called predators that something is other animals. Many animals spend their lives in danger of being captured by predators that are well adapted for hunting. Their arsenal of weapons includes sharp eyesight, great speed, and long claws or talons. But animals that are hunted are not defenseless. They can escape by flying or running away or by hiding in burrows; a few pretend to be dead.

Among the more effective defenses against predators are camouflage, bluffing, mimicking

the appearance of a plant, and imitating the behavior of more dangerous animals.

The colors of certain Arctic animals change to
match the surrounding landscape during different seasons. White in winter, brown in summer, this camouflage makes the animals less
distinguishable from their surroundings. Other
animals, because of their shapes and colors, become nearly invisible when they stand or rest in
positions that help their bodies look like leaves
or twigs. One of the animals shown below, the
silkworm moth, uses another defense: a star-

tling display. When threatened, it flashes open
its wings to show bright colors and large spots
that resemble eyes. Because these eyespots
mimic the eyes of large predators, they scare
away any attacking bird.

The willow ptarmigan *(top)* changes its feathers season-
ally, while the New Guinea cicada, Indian leaf bug, leaf
katydid, silkworm moth, stick-mimicking mantis, and
Asian horned toad *(bottom, left to right)* try to blend into
the background to improve their chances for survival.

Why Do Some Animals Imitate Their Surroundings?

Some animals rely on their camouflage to avoid predators. Camouflage may include coloring that blends with a background or having a shape that resembles that of another object. Each of the 14 animals hidden in this picture has a body shape and coloring that blend in with tree branches, leaves, or the forest floor. But colors and shapes alone are not enough. Predators can easily spot moving prey. If a potential prey moves, it likely will be seen by the predator. That's why animals that are camouflaged stay still when predators are near. The animals on these pages are symbolically grouped together. They actually live in different regions of the world, not in the same forest.

① Grasshopper
② Katydid
③ Australian brown newt
④ Stick insect
⑤ Nightjar
⑥ Asian horned toad
⑦ Katydid
⑧ Regal moth
⑨ Indian leaf bug
⑩ Leaf butterfly
⑪ Grasshopper
⑫ Bush katydid
⑬ Katydid
⑭ Yellow-tipped prominent moth

When Is a Bee Not a Bee?

Several kinds of harmless insects that have no stingers look like bees that can inflict a painful sting. This disguise helps protect the mimics from predators. In an experiment, scientists discovered that mimicry works only if the predator is fooled and only if the predator has already learned to avoid bees. These illustrations show how a southern toad learns this lesson.

① **A toad usually** eats anything that wiggles. This southern toad has never been stung by a bumblebee. When it sees a harmless robber fly, a bumblebee look-alike, it snaps it up immediately.

② **The toad spots** a bumblebee next. Without prior experience with bumblebees, the toad eats it but gets stung and spits out the bee.

Stingers and their mimics

The creatures on the previous two pages are camouflaged in ways that make it hard for predators to see them. Some insects, like the ones shown at right, are brightly colored and stand out from their surroundings, and predators can see them easily. Even so, their deceptive guises are at work. Bees and wasps sting, and their colors and patterns remind predators to leave them alone. Some harmless insects have evolved colors, patterns, and shapes that make them resemble stinging bees or wasps. The mimic insects can also make buzzing sounds like those of bees and wasps to warn off wary predators. The mimics' buzzing, stripes, and color patterns clearly send a "DON'T EAT ME" signal to predators.

A striped drone fly *(top)* looks similar to a honeybee.

④ **The toad ducks** its head, having learned a valuable lesson. From now on, the toad ignores any mimic that looks somewhat like a bee. The mimic's protection comes from its shape and coloring, but also from the toad's experience with a stinging bee. For the toad, once bitten, always shy.

③ **When a second** bumblebee flies near, the toad sees it but makes no attempt whatsoever to snap at it.

iger long-horned beetle *(top)* mimics a yellow jacket.

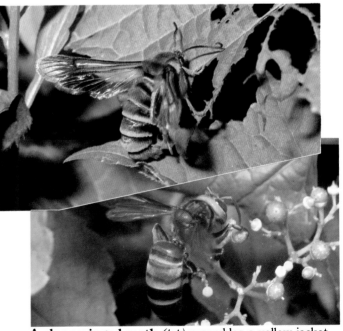

A clear-winged moth *(top)* resembles a yellow jacket.

Why Do Green Frogs Turn Brown?

When a tree frog is warmed by the sun, it looks green. A frog's skin has two layers, the epidermis and the dermis. The dermis contains color-producing cells: chromatophores, containing yellow and red pigments; iridophores, containing crystal platelets; and cells that contain brown and black pigments. The cells absorb most light colors, but the platelets scatter and reflect blue light back through the yellow pigment to produce green.

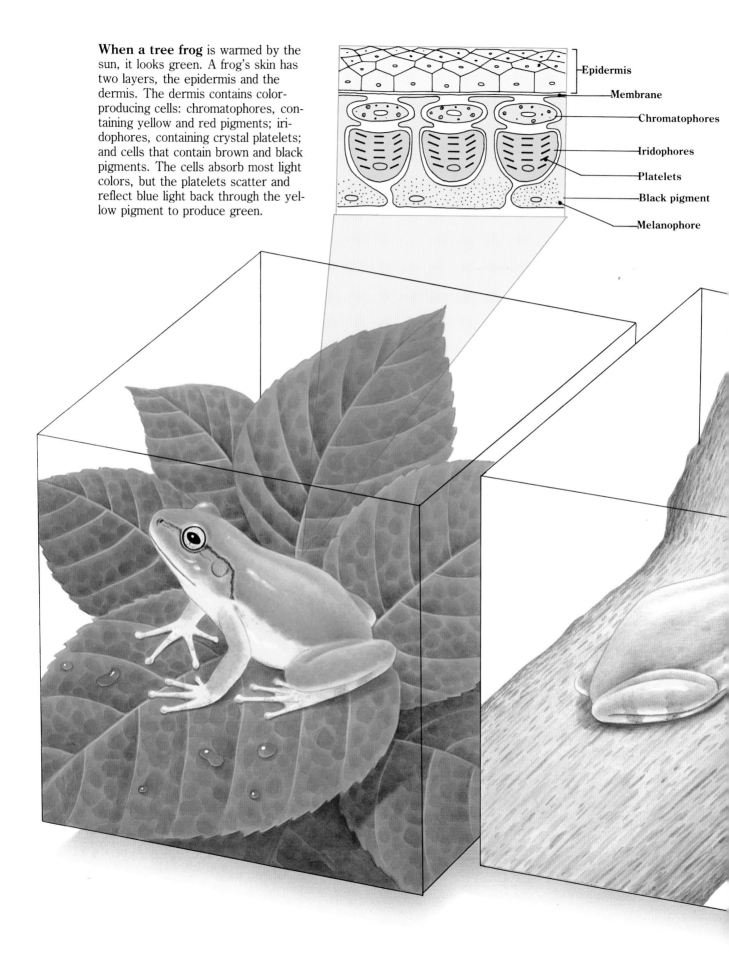

Epidermis
Membrane
Chromatophores
Iridophores
Platelets
Black pigment
Melanophore

The tree frog shown here and some other amphibians can change color as a means of protection. The tree frog may change its color to green when it sits among green leaves or to a mottled brown when it moves onto brown leaves. This protective coloring makes it hard for predators to see the frog. As an added benefit, the ability to change color also makes it more difficult for flies, beetles, and other prey to see the frog in time for them to escape being eaten.

The tree frog also adjusts its body temperature by changing color. On a hot, dry afternoon, a tree frog may find a light-colored place on which to perch. Its skin turns a lighter color and reflects sunlight, cooling the frog. When the air becomes cool and damp, the frog's skin turns darker and absorbs heat.

The changes in color are controlled by the pituitary gland embedded in the brain. The gland works like an internal thermostat and sends chemical signals to special skin cells called chromatophores. The cells work as shown below.

When the tree frog gets cold, chemical signals cause the iridophores to contract, disrupting the stacking of the platelets and making the black pigment disperse throughout the melanophore. Light cannot get through to the crystal platelets to be reflected. Yellow and black pigments create brown.

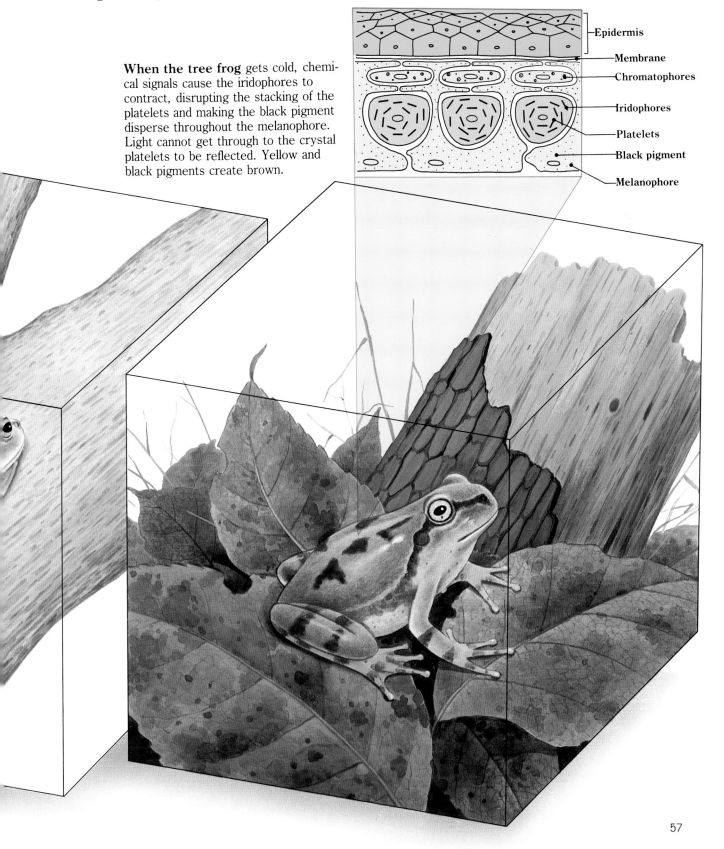

Epidermis
Membrane
Chromatophores
Iridophores
Platelets
Black pigment
Melanophore

Why Do Some Animals Change Color with the Seasons?

Winter

Spring

Do hares recognize the seasons?

Until recently researchers thought the color change in a snowshoe hare's fur was started by seasonal changes. Now they have proved that theory wrong. In a yearlong laboratory test, several white hares lived in hutches painted white inside to resemble snow. Others lived in hutches with brown interiors, the color of their summer habitat. The lights were kept on for 10 hours each "day," and the air was cooled and heated to match Arctic temperatures. The results were a surprise: All the hares remained white—no matter what their surroundings *(bottom right)*. In the wild, snowshoe hares began to turn brown late in February *(top right)*.

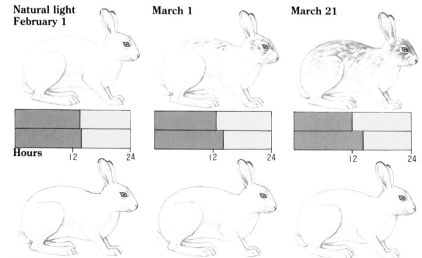

Natural light
February 1

March 1

March 21

Hours   12   24

12   24

12   24

Artificial light

Spring equinox, March 21

Some Arctic animals have camouflaged coats for winter and for summer. In winter, their white coats match the white landscape of snow. As spring arrives and brown patches of ground appear beneath the melting snow, their coats begin to turn brown. In the fall, their coats change back to white again.

Whether it happens to a bird or a mammal, changing colors means molting. During molt, new coats grow and old ones are shed. Rock ptarmigans, ermines, and snowshoe hares *(below, top to bottom)* show their coats in different seasons.

Summer

Fall

Daylight affects color change

In the second phase of the experiment, researchers placed two groups of brown snowshoe hares into hutches in late summer. They kept the laboratory at one steady warm temperature. For one group of hares, the lights stayed on for 14 hours a day. For the other group, the lights matched the hours of daylight in the Arctic. Gradually, as the length of the artificial days shortened, the hares began to change from brown to white. Clearly, the color changes in snowshoe hares are triggered by the spring and fall equinoxes—the two days a year that have exactly 12 hours of daylight and 12 hours of darkness.

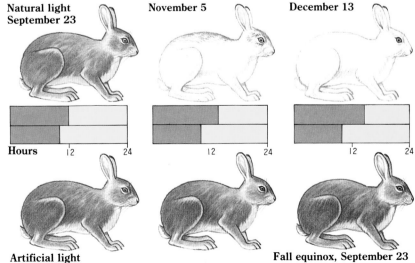

Natural light
September 23

November 5

December 13

Hours

Artificial light

Fall equinox, September 23

Why Do Springboks Jump?

Springboks and many other types of gazelles in Africa leap as high as 10 feet off the ground. While they are in the air, their legs stay stiff, their heads are lowered, and their bodies curve. This special kind of leaping is called stotting.

Researchers disagree why animals stot. According to one theory, stotting warns the cheetah or any other predator that it has been seen. Another theory holds that a gazelle's stotting signals to other gazelles that danger is near. Yet others think the animals stot so that they can see what is around them better, or they may stot for different reasons at different times.

Its back arched, its head down, its hooves drawn together, a stotting springbok warns the herd that a cheetah lurks nearby. This high leap may also alert the cheetah that it has been seen and discourage further hunting. The fleeing springbok at left provides another warning signal for the herd: the white patch on its rump.

Other warning signals

Animals that live in herds and keep their heads down while feeding need to protect themselves from enemies sneaking up on them. Because their eyes are on the sides of their heads, these animals see all around them even when they are eating. But that is not their only protection. When the herd is grazing, one animal at a time raises its head and keeps a lookout. If any member of the herd sees or smells anything suspicious, the white hairs on its rump rise up, silently signaling danger. When one herd member flees, the rest follow. The white rump markings help the lead animals guide the ones behind.

The white-tailed deer of North America raises its tail and its rump hair when it senses danger. This white flag makes the warning easier to see.

The pronghorn lives in North America's grasslands. Of all antelopes, it has the most distinct white markings with which to signal danger.

Why Does a Rattlesnake Make Noise?

A rattlesnake's rattling noise is part of its defense against attackers. When it feels threatened, the snake raises its head and shakes its tail rapidly. This warning rattle often startles the enemy, and that gives the snake enough time to escape and avoid having to fight. It may also serve to divert the enemy's first strike to the snake's tail instead of its head. When a rattlesnake is attacking prey, it raises its tail but does not shake its rattle.

Defensive behavior

Many snakes, poisonous and nonpoisonous, behave in threatening ways to protect themselves. Some harmless snakes have nearly the same patterns as poisonous ones and thus are left alone. When one kind of harmless snake makes its head wider, it looks like a pit viper. Poisonous snakes also might flatten their necks, make noises, or swell their bodies.

The saw-scaled viper, a poisonous Southwest Asian snake, scrapes its scales to sound a warning.

When a king cobra of Southeast Asia raises its head in a threat, its neck flares out like a hood. A king cobra may grow to 18 feet and can raise a fourth of its body in threat.

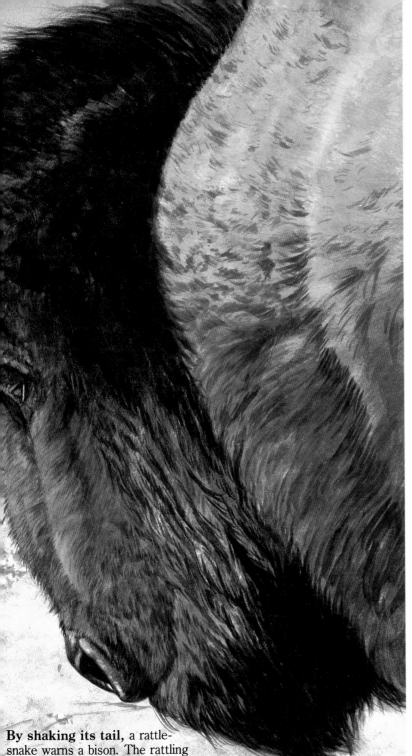

Scaly rattles

The rattlesnake's rattle, at the tip of its tail, is formed from large, hollow scales that clatter together when the snake shakes its tail. These special scales are the only ones that are not discarded when the snake sheds its scale-covered skin, or molts. Each time the snake molts, more rattles may develop.

Growth of a rattler's tail

A young rattlesnake slithers out of skin it has outgrown.

Unlike most snakes, the rattlesnake does not lay eggs. It gives birth to live young. A newborn has no rattle, but as it grows it sheds its skin repeatedly and rattles develop. A rattlesnake may shed many times a year; however, the number of scales in its rattle is not an indication of its age.

By shaking its tail, a rattlesnake warns a bison. The rattling noise can make even large animals treat the snake with caution.

The disturbed boomslang of southwestern Africa inflates its throat to scare an attacker. If it inflates its entire body, it almost doubles in size. Fangs at the back of its mouth release a deadly poison.

An eastern mud snake of North America can startle its captor by stabbing it with its pointed tail. The harmless mud snake then quickly escapes.

What Is the Purpose of Eyespots?

Many animals have eyespots, or patterns that look like eyes, somewhere on their bodies, but they usually keep them hidden. When the animal is threatened, it suddenly reveals its eyespots. The attacker may be so startled that the animal with the eyespots has time to escape.

Other animals have eyespots near their back ends, making the rear look like the head. Predators attacking such an animal expect it to flee in one direction, but instead it escapes in another.

When threatened, an adult luna moth flashes open its hind wings and reveals the eyespots underneath. The startled bird may fly away or be so confused that the moth has time to escape.

Eyespots that deter predators

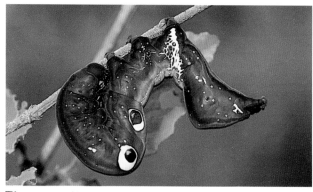

The caterpillar of the Malayan butterfly twists its body to reveal its eyespots, confusing attackers.

To a bird, this may look like the head of a snake. It is actually the tail of a moth larva with big eyespots.

Are birds fooled by eyespots?

To test whether eyespots frighten birds, a scientist conducted an experiment by placing worms on a specially prepared box. When a bird approached to snatch a worm, the scientist turned on a light inside the box to reveal one of the patterns at right. He discovered that birds were startled more by a circle than by an equal or a plus sign. The circles that resembled staring, unblinking eyes startled the birds the most. This experiment supports the theory that eyespots alarm predators.

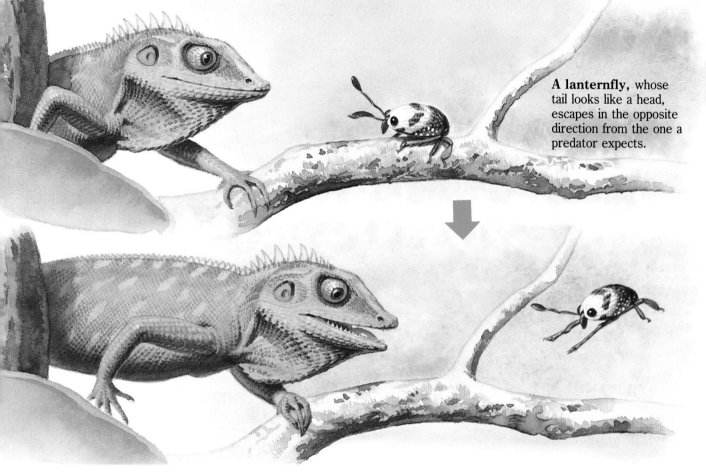

A lanternfly, whose tail looks like a head, escapes in the opposite direction from the one a predator expects.

Eyespots that help an escape

A bird may have mistakenly pecked at the eyespot on the wing of this grayling butterfly.

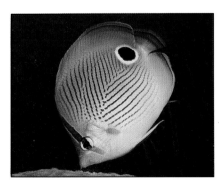

A butterfly fish escapes when a predator attacks the flashy eyespot on its tail instead of its true eye.

The white eyespots at the end of this butterfly's tail make the tail look like the head.

Why Are Poisonous Frogs So Bright?

Some frogs of Central and South America secrete a deadly poison often used by Indians of Colombia for poison arrows and darts. The frogs have come to be called dart-poison frogs, and their exceptionally bright coloring helps both the frogs and the would-be predators.

Predators quickly learn that bright frogs taste terrible. The frogs' coloring then protects the frogs from future attacks and the predators from bitter, even fatal meals.

Bright colors also help other poisonous animals. Some animals reveal bright areas on their bodies to startle or intimidate attackers, then escape.

Bright frogs of the genus *Dendrobates*

Dendrobates pumilio

Dendrobates histrionicus

Dendrobates pumilio

Dendrobates histrionicus

Dendrobates pumilio

Dendrobates lehmanni

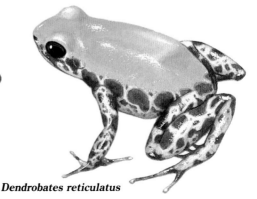

Dendrobates quinquevittatus   *Dendrobates auratus*   *Dendrobates reticulatus*

A bird that caught a dart-poison frog in its beak quickly spits it out. The bird will remember to avoid such a brightly colored, foul-tasting frog in the future.

Dendrobates pumilio

Dendrobates leucomelas

Dendrobates granuliferus

The menacing pose of a newt

Some poisonous amphibians are not as visible as the dart-poison frogs. When seen from above, the dark topside of the California newt, for example, blends in with the ground covering. But when under attack, the newt strikes a strange pose to reveal the bright coloring on its underside. The sudden flash of color scares the predator or warns it to stay away from this unpleasant meal.

Why Do Some Harmless Butterflies Mimic Poisonous Ones?

Many harmless butterflies fool predators because they look like poisonous ones. This survival technique, called Batesian mimicry, is also found in certain flies and moths that resemble wasps and bees.

Some butterflies are poisonous because as caterpillars they eat poisonous plants. The poison stays in their bodies even after they become butterflies. Other species of butterflies produce their own poison. Predators that eat one of these will feel ill and will not attack another one, and will avoid harmless butterflies that resemble poisonous ones.

Birds and poisonous butterflies

A young bird that is inexperienced does not know the coloration and markings of poisonous butterflies and may capture and eat one.

After swallowing the vile-tasting butterfly, the poisoned bird vomits but survives.

The bird learns from this not to eat that kind of butterfly again. It even stops catching other butterflies that resemble the poisonous kind.

Harmful and harmless butterflies

The butterflies in the top row are poisonous. The ones below are harmless, but their colors and patterns closely resemble those of the harmful ones. Henry Bates discovered this kind of mimicry while he was in Brazil in the 1850s.

Poisonous milkweed butterfly

Poisonous crow butterfly

Nonpoisonous mimics

Nonpoisonous mimics

Nonpoisonous mimics

Mimicry among poisonous butterflies

Different species of poisonous butterflies sometimes resemble each other. This is an advantage to the butterflies because predators have to learn to avoid only one pattern, not several different ones. As a result, each species of butterfly is attacked less often. In the pairs of poisonous butterflies shown below, those on the left belong to one species and those on the right belong to another. Throughout Central and South America the members of each of these species have different patterns, but in any one location members of both species look very much alike. This is called Müllerian mimicry. Certain wasps and bees also exhibit this form of mimicry.

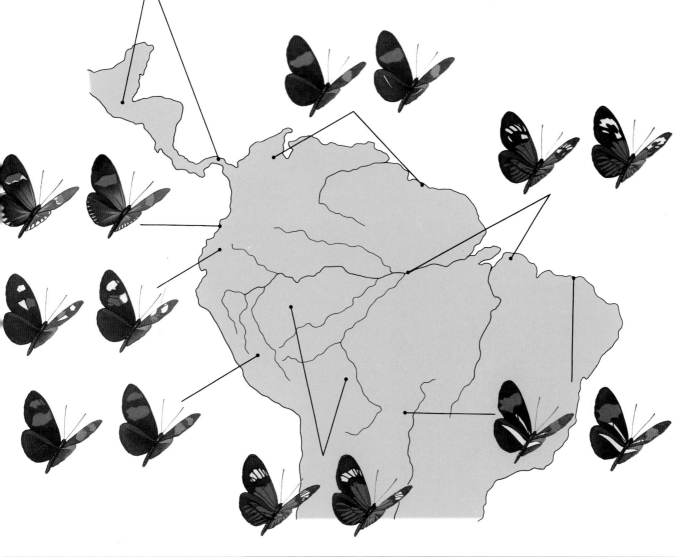

Mimicry among insects

Different species of insects living in the same region can have almost identical coloring and markings. These yellow and black insects all live in Africa, while the red and black insects live in Southeast Asia. Their bright appearance warns predators to keep away. Both Batesian and Müllerian mimicry are present here, because some of these insects are poisonous and others are not.

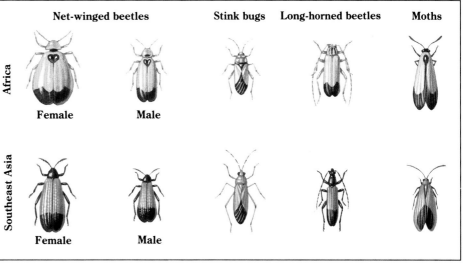

	Net-winged beetles		Stink bugs	Long-horned beetles	Moths
Africa	Female	Male			
Southeast Asia	Female	Male			

Why Are Clown Fish Safe from Stings?

Sea anemones are predatory animals. They catch their prey, mostly crustaceans and fish, by paralyzing them with their tentacles, which contain stinging cells. When a fish is caught, the sea anemone passes it along to its mouth with its tentacles and eats it. But the clown fish safely lives among the sea anemone's tentacles.

A clown fish is not born with protection from an anemone's stings, but slowly builds up a resistance. When a clown fish first approaches a sea anemone, it carefully touches its tail or fins to the anemone's tentacles and then pulls quickly away. After about an hour of repeated touching, the anemone has added a layer of mucus to the clown fish's own mucus coating. Any time thereafter when the anemone's tentacles touch the clown fish, they are not stimulated to sting.

Protective mucus layer

The life of a clown fish

The female lays its eggs on a rock near a sea anemone. The male guards them while the female patrols the area.

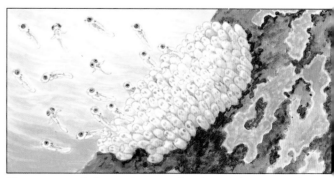

About a week later the eggs hatch and the young rise to the surface to swim about.

The clown fish protects the sea anemone by driving off butterfly-fish, which bite at parts of the tentacles that do not sting. With its bright coloring, the clown fish attracts prey to the sea anemone and shares in the catch.

The sea anemone protects the clown fish from predators. The clown fish helps the sea anemone in return, cleaning away sand and debris and separating the tentacles to allow more sunlight to reach the algae and seaweed, which are also food for the sea anemone.

In seven days the young develop a mucus covering and bright coloration and swim down to find a sea anemone.

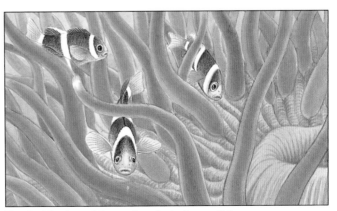

Probably lured by a chemical given off by a sea anemone, the young fish begin living among its tentacles.

How Can Wingless Animals Glide?

Some animals that make their homes high up in trees move swiftly from place to place by gliding. They are not agile on the ground and are easy prey there. But in the air they control their flight, making turns to avoid small branches and landing on choice spots.

These so-called flying animals have limbs that can function like parachutes or wings. When they glide, they change the shape of these body parts into aerodynamic extensions. They can't actually fly, but they can glide in a sloping descent instead of falling.

Colugo, or flying lemur. With the largest gliding flap of all mammals, this lemur can travel 100 yards through the air.

Flying dragon or flying lizard. Native to Southeast Asia, this reptile lives in trees. Its long ribs support a web of skin on each side. The webs act like glider wings and help the dragon escape predators.

Flying gecko. A membrane that stretches out on both sides of its body, a flat tail, and webs between its toes enable this gecko to glide.

Flying frog. When a flying frog leaps from tree to tree, the large webs between its toes act as parachutes to slow its descent.

Giant flying squirrel

The giant flying squirrel has an exceptionally bushy tail plus a membrane that stretches between its legs. The flying squirrel climbs up high on one tree then shoves off for a spot lower down on a nearby trunk. Sometimes it glides 100 yards or more. It steers by dipping one shoulder or the other and moving its tail like a rudder. Coming in for a landing, it raises its body and tail to slow down. Over and over the squirrel climbs and glides to reach its destination.

Why Do Fish Swim in Schools?

Many different kinds of fish swim in large groups called schools as a means of protection. For any small fish, being a member of a large group reduces the risk of getting eaten. Because many fish are keeping a lookout for danger, a school of fish is likely to notice a predator sooner than a single fish will.

Another reason for forming schools may involve the search for food. With its many eyes, the school can more easily detect food than can a single fish. A school also has a better chance than a single fish has of capturing prey.

A predator drives into a school. The small fish quickly scatter. Because of the movement and confusion, the predator often cannot pick out a single fish to attack before they all escape. If a fish does not keep up with the school, the predator stands a good chance of capturing it.

Fish that form schools are slower than predators, but they can dart and turn much faster. When attacked, a school escapes in a flash by splitting and rejoining behind the predator.

A school of small fish discovered by a predator swims as a group to try to escape, but generally the fish cannot swim as fast as the predator. Their defense lies in agility, not speed.

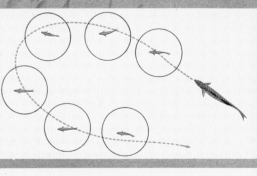

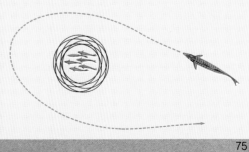

Swimming alone or in a school

Visibility under water is limited and predators can only see prey within a certain distance *(indicated by circles)*. If six fish are spread throughout the ocean, a predator's chances of finding any one of them are pretty good. If they are grouped together, the chances of any one of them getting caught drop to only one in six. The chances of escape improve as the number of fish in a school increases.

How Do Hermit Crabs Find New Shells?

Hermit crabs live in the empty shells of other shellfish. When a hermit crab outgrows its shell or the shell becomes weak, it searches for a larger or stronger one. Sometimes, the crab finds an empty shell. But often, it steals the shell of another hermit crab or of a shellfish. It may seem cruel for one hermit crab to take the home of another, but most of the time the evicted crab moves into the shell of its invader. The shellfish is not as fortunate. After the crab removes the defenseless creature from its shell, the crab usually eats it.

Spying a larger shell, an invading hermit crab grips the claws of the owner and drags it from its dwelling.

Taking over a new shell

Hermit crabs are not easily pulled out of their shells. When threatened, they move far back into their homes and hang on stubbornly. But one hermit crab knows how to make another one leave. It bangs its shell against the other crab's shell. That disturbs the other crab, which sometimes simply leaves its shell. Other times it pokes out its head and the attacking crab yanks it all the way out. The loser usually moves into the shell abandoned by the attacker. The shell might fit better, but if the home is too snug, the crab searches for a new one. It must move quickly though. Without its shell, a hermit crab is easy prey for hungry fish.

An invader knocks against a larger shell, disturbing the hiding crab.

Using the stronger claw, the invader flings the victim from its shell.

76

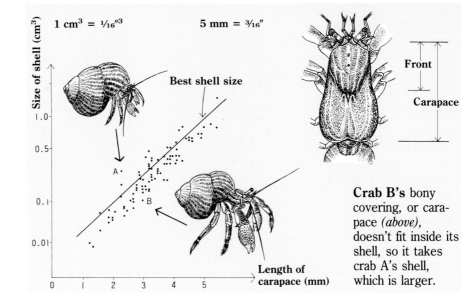

Two hermit crabs force a shellfish from its home. Later, the crabs will fight for the empty shell.

Tiny limbs at the end of the crab's body and smaller middle legs grasp the shell to hold the crab inside.

▼ **A hermit crab** makes sure it will fit in an empty shell by measuring the width with its claws.

The invader moves in. The evicted crab takes the invader's old home.

Size of shell (cm³)

1 cm³ = 1/16″³   5 mm = 3/16″

Best shell size

A

B

1.0

0.5

0.1

0.01

0   1   2   3   4   5

Length of carapace (mm)

Front

Carapace

Crab B's bony covering, or carapace *(above)*, doesn't fit inside its shell, so it takes crab A's shell, which is larger.

Why Do Hermit Crabs Carry Sea Anemones?

Hermit crabs usually hide from enemies by pulling back into their shells. But even a shell is not strong enough to stop a hungry sea creature like an octopus. To protect itself from this and other deadly predators, the hermit crab carries a sea anemone on its back. With its stinging tentacles, the anemone is armed against any predator that might consider it as a meal.

This close partnership also helps the sea anemone. Ordinarily, an anemone attaches itself to a rock or shell and stays put. But when a hermit crab attaches an anemone to its shell, the anemone gets a ride to new feeding grounds every day.

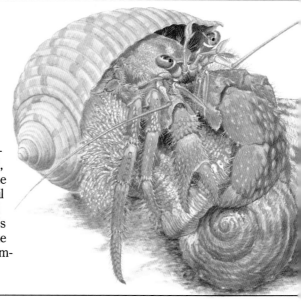

A generous host, the hermit crab can support several sea anemones at once, sometimes as many as seven or eight.

A crab with sea anemones on its shell walks safely past an octopus. The predator has learned from painful experience not to touch the anemone's stinging tentacles.

Without a sea anemone, a hermit crab snared in the grip of an octopus is defenseless. The octopus's mouth can grind up the crab's shell.

Moving an anemone

When a hermit crab outgrows its shell, it moves to a new one. If it has anemones on its shell, the crab also takes them along. A person trying to pry an anemone off a hermit crab's shell would have a tough time. Sea anemones hold on to their supports with powerful suction disks at their bases. Any attempt to move a sea anemone by force causes the anemone to contract into a tight mound that cannot be moved. But when the crab tries, it gently massages the anemone with its claws until the anemone relaxes, grows limp, and loosens its grip. Then the crab plucks the anemone off its shell and carries it in its claws to their new home.

Safely tucked inside its new shell, the crab prods the sea anemone until it releases its old home. The crab is not harmed by the poison in the anemone's tentacles.

▼ **A crab** plugs its shell entrance with its big claw. The anemone adds further protection.

◄ **Towering over** the crab, this large sea anemone eventually may grow to cover the shell.

If the anemone was put on upside down, it rights itself, moves to a good position, and then sticks firmly in place.

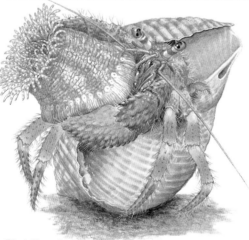

Holding it between its claws, the crab places the sea anemone on its new shell. Sometimes the anemone is upside down.

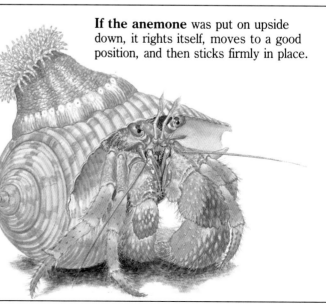

Why Does a Lizard Break Its Tail?

Many lizards are clever escape artists. When a predator grabs the tail of one of these lizards, such as the five-lined skink shown here, the lizard breaks its tail off. The discarded part of the tail wriggles wildly and distracts the attacker long enough so the lizard can scurry away to safety.

It doesn't hurt the lizard to lose its tail, because it has a built-in snap-off point. When an attacker grabs the tail, the lizard contracts its tail muscles at this special place and the tail breaks cleanly. The attacker may eat the broken-off piece.

As soon as the lizard drops its tail, a new one begins to grow. A lizard can reproduce a new tail as many times as needed. This process of growing new body parts is called regeneration.

A lizard's tail doesn't break just anywhere; it has a special place where the bones and tissue pull apart easily.

Animals that grow new parts

Crabs, stick insects, and lugworms are among the many creatures that drop off parts of their bodies to defend themselves from an enemy's attack. They simply contract muscles to cause the break. These animals can get along fine without the body parts that they leave behind.

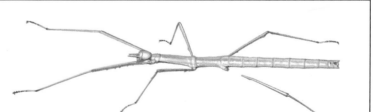

Thin as a matchstick, the stick insect usually isn't seen by its enemies because it blends in with the plant it is standing on. If it does get caught, the insect easily discards a leg.

If a crab is in great danger and cannot escape by any other means, it detaches one of its claws to get away.

The lugworm can survive a fierce attack by separating from its hind region. The severed hind part will grow into a new worm.

The tail breaks where the bone is brittle
and snaps off painlessly. As the tail drops
off, a thin, clear film covers the stump and
stops the loss of blood. The healing process
begins immediately.

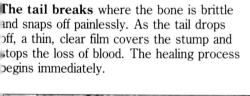

A lizard with its original tail intact

A lizard in the process of growing a new tail

Can a Squid Fly?

Flying squid can flee from an enemy faster than almost any other animal in the sea. The squid's streamlined, torpedo-shaped body allows it to swim easily and smoothly. By forcing streams of water through a built-in funnel under its head, this marine rocket can jet up and out of the sea as fast as 35 miles per hour. Squid propel themselves upward with such force that some have been known to land on the decks of ships. Yet these sea racers can slow to a snail's pace, especially when they are moving in to surprise prey.

In the air, the squid keeps on course with the arrowhead-shaped fin at the tip of its body. This fin acts as a balancing device. The squid's eight muscular arms and two long tentacles fan out like wings. Scientists think that a sticky film fills the space between the outstretched limbs. The film creates a surface that lifts and supports the gliding creature.

The squid has other advantages over its predators. It has excellent eyesight and can spot an attacker while it is yet some distance away. But should a predator get too close, the squid has an emergency backup. It releases a thick, black spray of ink that temporarily distracts the enemy while the squid makes a quick getaway.

Rocketing out of the ocean to escape a predator, flying squid can cover a distance of 150 feet or more in a single glide.

The flying squid's design

Like the Concorde supersonic jet, the flying squid is shaped perfectly for fast takeoffs. The squid is thrust upward by fast-moving currents of water and air that stream backward along its body. The squid's spread-out limbs act like the jet's delta-shaped wings and give it the lift it needs to glide. Much like the jet's rear fin and rudder, the fin at the tip of the squid stabilizes its flight.

An airborne squid   **The Concorde**

How Does a Plover Outfox a Fox?

Plovers are famous for protecting their young by tricking predators. When a fox or other enemy heads toward the nest, the plover appears to be injured. The predator sees the bird and follows it. As soon as the enemy has been led a safe distance from the nest, the bird stops faking injury and flies away.

It is easy to believe that plovers act injured on purpose to protect their chicks, but scientists doubt that birds can think that way. Perhaps instinct takes over and the plover wants to protect itself by flying away at the same time that it wants to protect its eggs or chicks. Neither of these instincts is stronger than the other, so the plover acts in a confused way—and accidentally tricks the predator. Once the predator is too far away to see the nest, the plover's instinct to protect itself becomes stronger than the instinct to protect the nest and the plover flies away.

The plover spots a fox hunting dangerously close to its nestling chicks. Immediately it rises and slowly moves away from its young.

Other ways of bluffing

Opossums and certain snakes and beetles are just some of the creatures that bluff their way out of dangerous situations. Many predators—cats, lizards, and frogs, for example—attack only living, moving animals. An animal that holds still as if it were dead often escapes attack. If the prey stays motionless long enough, the attacker may not be able to find it. Even if it sees its prey, the attacker may lose interest. Then the bluffer hurriedly escapes.

Once the plover has led the fox far from the nest, it suddenly flies to safety. The fox never sees the nest and doesn't know it is there, so the chicks are safe for now.

As it moves away from the nest, the plover utters pitiful cries and bends and flaps one of its wings as if it were hurt. This activity captures the attention of the fox, which stalks the "injured" bird.

Opossum

Hognose snake

Snout beetle

Why Do Gobies and Shrimp Make Good Roommates?

Goby fish and snapping shrimp rely on a buddy system for survival. They stay close together near a nesting hole the shrimp has dug in sand in shallow waters. When an enemy approaches, the sharp-eyed goby spots it and quickly enters the shrimp's nesting hole. The goby's movement warns the shrimp of the danger and the shrimp follows behind. The goby benefits from the shrimp's hard work by having a ready-made escape hatch. But the shrimp benefits from the partnership too. Because it is timid and cannot see very well, the shrimp depends on the goby to spot predators. The shrimp also feeds on scraps of food left over from the goby's meal.

① **Peering out** from its hiding place in the shrimp's burrow, the goby looks all around to see if any danger is near. The shrimp stays in contact with the goby at all times by resting one of its antennae on the fish.

Goby and shrimp partners

Early in their lives, gobies search for young shrimp beginning to dig their tunnel homes. If gobies fail to find partners quickly, they will be eaten by predators. In an area where the gobies outnumber the shrimp, competition among gobies looking for a hole can get fierce. Sometimes, two gobies share a single burrow. Biologists have identified more than 30 kinds of gobies that have partnerships with shrimp. A few of these gobies are shown at the right.

Sand goby lives with snapping shrimp.

The iridescent naked goby seeks food

③ **The ever-watchful goby** catches sight of a threatening fish. Immediately the goby flicks its tail in rapid bursts, a signal that warns the shrimp to hide.

② **If the area** appears safe, the goby and shrimp venture farther out of the hole. The goby searches for food that is close to the nest, and the shrimp removes sand from the entrance to its burrow.

④ **The goby dives** into the hole head-first, while the shrimp races in backwards. Both remain in the hole until the goby sees that it is safe to come out again to search for food.

Striped shrimp and goby stay close together.

Ginsburg's gobies share a hole with a snapping shrimp.

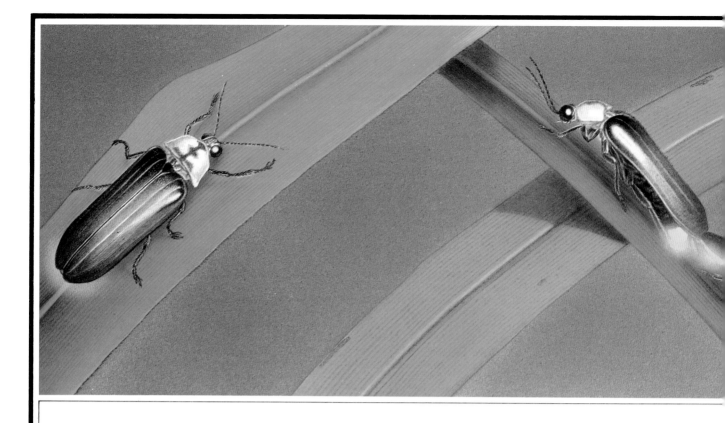

3
Mating and Parenting

Animals face two crucial challenges in life: surviving to adulthood and reproducing their species. To survive, an animal must find food and escape predators and overcome disease and dangers from natural elements, such as cold and drought. To reproduce, the eggs of the female must be fertilized by the sperm of a male.

Not all creatures have to meet for fertilization to occur. Among small creatures in oceans and lakes, for example, the females release their eggs and the males release their sperm into the water, where they are carried by currents. Rel-

tively few of the eggs are fertilized, yet enough
re to ensure that the species will continue to ex-
st. But for most animals, the males and females
nust find a mate.

Animals have many different ways of finding
nates. Some sing or make strange sounds to at-
ract each other. Others release special odors or
lash lights. Once potential mates have found
each other, they must coordinate their sexual
drives so that both partners are ready to mate at
he same time. A few animals must even avoid
provoking an attack from a potential mate.

After the eggs are laid or the young are born,
parenting begins. Female mammals nurse and
defend their offspring. Adults also protect their
young in the world of birds, a few fish, insects,
amphibians, and reptiles—all so that the species
are able to survive.

Finding mates or offspring can be tricky. Fireflies
(above) signal with light to attract each other, while penguins recognize their chicks in a group by their voices.

How Do Male Spiders Court Females?

A spider lurking in its web looks upon anything wiggling the strands as either a meal or an enemy. That can make mating tricky. Although they are usually smaller than females, male spiders do all the courting. And for many types of spiders, the male must walk on the female's web to reach her. To keep from being attacked, he gently jiggles her web to avoid surprising her and to make sure she is at home. Next comes a complicated courtship routine that is different for each species. The various types of behavior help ensure that the male approaches only females of his own species and that he can safely finish mating.

A male flytrap spider dances in front of a female by waving his front legs up and down. Each species of flytrap spider dances in a slightly different way.

A male running spider presents a female with prey he has captured. While she is distracted by the gift, he safely mates with her. Nursery web spiders—which make a silken tent for their young—also court with gifts.

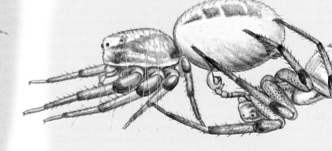

A male crab spider loops silk over the female's legs so he will not be attacked while mating. After he leaves, the female easily breaks free.

Mating in a web-spinning species

After a male spider molts for the last time, he reaches sexual maturity. Now he looks different from the females and is capable of mating. First, however, he must spin a small web within his main web to collect sperm from his genital opening. Then he dips his pedipalps into the small web to retrieve the sperm. Pedipalps are small limbs just behind his fangs, and their tips have hollow chambers that hold the sperm. During mating, the spider uses his pedipalps to place sperm in the female's genital opening.

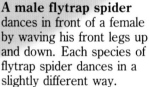

At maturity, a male spins a special sperm web in the middle of his main web.

The male drips sperm from his genital opening onto the sperm web.

Spiders that build webs sense when the web has caught something by feeling the vibrations produced by the struggling prey. A male garden spider or black widow intent on mating must make sure the female does not think he is prey. As he walks on her web, he sends a friendly greeting by tapping and plucking strands of silk with his legs. His body also twitches and vibrates in a special way. The female may still chase him off, but if she wants to mate, she returns the signals.

3 **After receiving** an answer from the female, the male slowly approaches the center of the web, continuing to send his vibrating signals. During the trip across the web, males of different species display different courting behavior.

1 **A male wiggles** to announce his arrival. If he receives no response, he may continue signaling for several days. He may even wait until a young female becomes sexually mature.

2 **A female** that has received a male's signals answers by jerking and twitching her body. If she is not interested in mating, she may attack or refuse to return his signals.

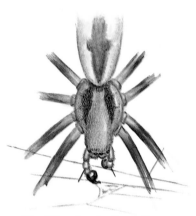

He fills the hollow tips of his pedipalps with sperm from the web.

After finding a female, he performs a courtship ritual unique to his species.

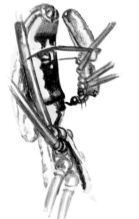

The male passes sperm to the genital pore on the female's body.

Why Do Fireflies Glow?

A male firefly sweeps his glowing tail through the air like a swinging flashlight, creating a blinking, yellow-green pattern of light. The female waits near the ground, twinkling in return. With this code of light, male and female fireflies find each other so they can mate. Fireflies produce this cool chemical light in special cells near the tip of their abdomens. Each species of firefly living in a particular area has its own pattern of light. People who study fireflies can identify over 130 types of fireflies around the world by their different flashing patterns.

▲ **A male Heike firefly** of Japan flashes about once per second. The female blinks back with alternating strong and weak flashes.

Communication among fireflies

Although there are many species of fireflies, the members of a particular one are able to find each other because each species in an area has a special pattern of flashes. The length and frequency of each flash and the flight pattern of the male as he flashes are part of the message. As males and females recognize each other, they may change the pattern of flashes. A male that has not located a mate blinks slowly. Females flash a response to the males' blinks, advertising their location. Once he sees a female, a male approaches and speeds up his pattern of blinks. Then the female flashes less often. The male's light also becomes dimmer, so that competing males will not home in on his beacon. Normally a female answers only males of her own species. But some females lure males of other species and eat them. Response to light is automatic. Female fireflies also react to artificial lights, even flashlights.

● **Fireflies exchange signals—10 p.m.**

| Male | In flight |
| Female | At rest |

● **Signals before mating—midnight**

| Male | In flight |
| Female | At rest |

Male princess fireflies become active around 10 p.m., skimming over the grass and blinking about once every second. The females begin to wink their lights on and off once every two to three seconds. About midnight, just before they mate, both males and females flash more frequently.

▲ **A male princess** firefly blinks rapidly as he circles a female. She responds with slower flashes.

▲ **The large male Genji** firefly blinks slowly, creating long streaks of light in the night sky.

Artificial
light

Female

Artificial
light

Female

● Fireflies exchange signals—8 p.m.

Male   In flight

Female   At rest

● Before mating—
9 p.m.

Male   In flight

Female   At rest

If a green light bulb is flashed on and off at the right intervals, a female princess firefly flashes in response, just as she would to a male. If the light flashes too fast, the female will not respond to each flash. If it is too slow, she adds an extra response between light flashes.

Male Genji fireflies search for females by flying in large groups and flashing their lights in unison. The females blink from the grass to attract the males. But unlike other species, Genji females do not respond to each male flash. Before mating, both males and females blink less often.

How Do Moths Find Each Other at Night?

Male moths usually cannot find females with their eyes in the dark, but they can find them with their antennae. Females release a special chemical odor, called a sex pheromone, into the air. Because of the sensitivity of their huge, feathery antennae, males can detect even a few molecules of this chemical miles away from the female. When a male detects the pheromone, he follows it to its source. When he arrives, he is sure to find a mature female because young female moths do not produce sex pheromones. And he will find the right kind of female moth, because the pheromone of each species contains a slightly different chemical mixture. A male usually responds only to pheromones created by the female of its own species.

Once he is close to her, the male can see the female; he can also find her by sensing the heat from her body.

The feathery antennae of a male giant silkworm moth have many tiny strands, each covered with pheromone sensors. With an antenna on each side of its head, a male moth can detect where the pheromone is coming from.

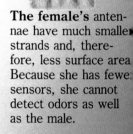

The female's antennae have much smaller strands and, therefore, less surface area. Because she has fewer sensors, she cannot detect odors as well as the male.

How a male moth finds a female

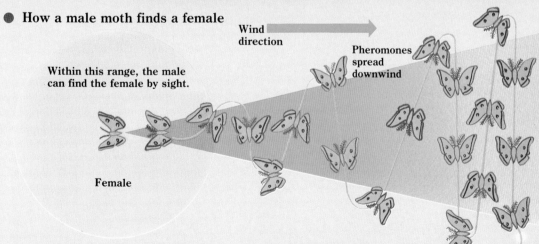

Wind direction

Pheromones spread downwind

Within this range, the male can find the female by sight.

Female

When a female matures, she begins releasing sex pheromones at night from the tip of her abdomen. Each species releases pheromones only at certain times of night, and each species has its own type of pheromone. That helps males to find females of the same species. The odor spreads and fades in the wind. Like a dog following a scent, the male moth flies upwind, zigging and zagging back and forth through the pheromone trail. He turns toward the antenna that senses the most pheromone molecules, and each turn brings him closer to the female. When he finally finds the female, they mate.

Why Do Crickets Chirp?

The field cricket of Taiwan lives in grassy plains and meadows and makes a call that sounds like "ri-i—ri-i."

Cricket trills that fill a summer evening with music come from an all-male choir. Each male calls to advertise his own territory. To other males this calling song means "back off," but to females it is very attractive. If a cricket of either sex responds by approaching, the singing male changes his song abruptly. A trespassing male is warned off by a shrill series of loud chirps—the fighting song. But a mature female gets a slow, soft song indicating the male's desire to mate. All cricket songs have distinct patterns and are sung at different speeds. Each type of cricket sings a unique set of songs, and females of one type of cricket respond only to the chirps from males of their own kind.

The northern cricket of Japan lives under rocks in dry river-beds. Its distinctive call is "chi-ri-ri-ri—chi-ri-ri-ri."

Calling song

Beginning in early evening, male crickets sing all night long. But they do not all sing at once. In any area where crickets have gathered, the males take turns calling. This prevents the males from trespassing on each other's territory. Scientists think the calls help males measure the distance between each other and, thus, to stay a certain distance apart. If a calling song is tape-recorded and then played back, a male stops chirping, moves a short distance away, and starts again. If a female approaches, the male then switches to the gentler courtship song.

Even if the males of the three types of crickets shown at left and below were to sing to this female at one time, she could pick out the one that was her own species by his song. She would approach and mate with only that male.

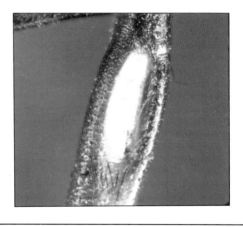

A cricket's "ears"

A cricket's "ears," the so-called tympanic membranes, are near the knees of the front legs. Each one is a pit covered with a thin, oval eardrum. Crickets can detect tiny differences in rhythm, but cannot separate pitches.

The Oriental garden cricket resides in cultivated fields and moors. Its call is "koro-koro-koro-ri."

How does a cricket sing?

A cricket chirps by rubbing its front wings together. It lifts these wings and scrapes the edge of the right one against a bumpy ridge in the middle of the left wing, which vibrates like a washboard stroked by fingers covered with thimbles. Each stroke produces one chirp. The male's song is a series of chirps.

Ridge on the left wing 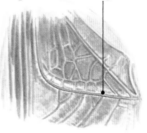   Scraper on the right wing

Courtship song or fighting song

If a male's calling song attracts a female, he will sing a courtship song. This quieter, slower set of chirps puts the female in the mood to mate. In some species, the courtship song may have two or three parts, each quieter than the one before. During mating the male may produce nothing but a soft ticking sound.

If a male intrudes on another male's turf, both sing a fighting song consisting of a long set of loud chirps. As they chirp, the battling males butt their heads together. When one gives up and leaves, the victor renews his calling song.

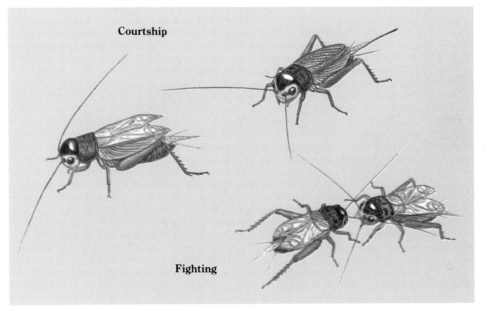

Courtship

Fighting

Why Do Birds Sing?

All of the world's 8,700 different bird species call, but only 5,000 sing. A bird's call repeats short sounds, like the "caw" of a crow, while a song has an organized pattern of sounds.

The males do almost all the singing, and a male's tune tells a lot about him: It reveals his maturity, his sex, and his species. In addition to singing a song unique to his species, he may sing in a local or regional dialect. Some males even add personal touches all their own. White-crowned sparrows and many other birds sing only a single, simple tune; others sing more complex tunes. The brown thrasher could perform all day and never repeat himself—he may know as many as 2,000 melodies.

No matter how many songs he has, a male's singing always serves two purposes: to attract females and to warn off males. A male's barrage of notes and trills during the mating season usually prevents other males from attempting to invade his territory.

An Asian warbler sings to claim his territory in a field.

A male warbler attacks any male trespassing on his territory. If he hasn't mated yet, he must maintain his territory in order to attract a female. If he has a mate that hasn't laid eggs yet, he must prevent the other males from mating with her.

A female feeds her chicks while the male defends their territory. A male Oriental great reed warbler takes no part in sitting on eggs but may help protect and feed the chicks of his first mate.

Do songbirds sing all the time?

In spring, many songbirds, such as the Oriental great reed warblers of Japan, migrate home from their winter quarters to choose territories. A male that arrives early can pick a lush spot with plenty of insects. Once he stakes out his homestead, he pours out a song lasting from dawn until after sunset (top right).

After males have divided a field into well-defended territories, the females return. A female investigates the field, listens to the songs, and checks out each male's realm. She is looking for a good territory as well as a mate. After mating, the female builds a nest while the male tirelessly patrols his borders, keeping other males away. He has little time for singing (center right).

Her egg laying done, the female will not mate again until next year. The male is free to sing once more and attract another female (bottom right). A female that returns late from migration may have to choose between a male that already has a mate and one with no mate but a poor territory. If territories differ greatly, she may choose the male with the better territory. Only about 20 percent of the males mate twice in a season.

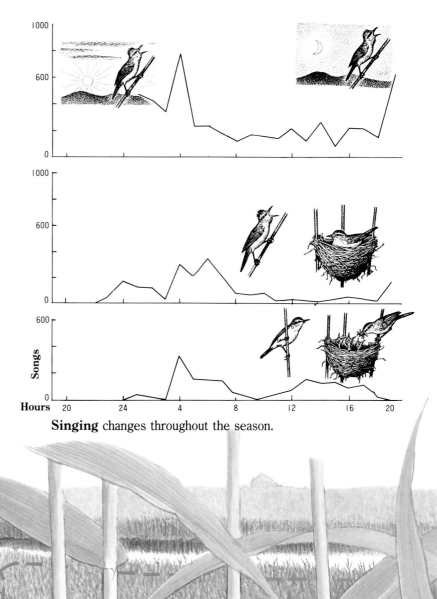

Singing changes throughout the season.

Singing loudly from a high perch, a male keeps watch over his territory. Except when he feeds in the grass, the male stays constantly on watch, reminding other males that his territory is taken.

After comparing territories, this female chose the number two spot in one male's realm. She shares food with the male, his first mate, and their young, but her family will fare better than if she had picked a male with a poor territory.

Why Do Bowerbirds Build Bowers?

Instead of singing to defend an area, a male bowerbird creates a territory. He clears a small patch of forest floor and decorates it with colorful objects and a twig structure called a bower. Some males even paint a bower's inside walls with berry juice or mud and saliva.

A bower looks a bit like a nest, but that is not its function; its only use is to attract females. A female selects her mate by the appeal of his bower. All 20 species of bowerbirds live in Australia and New Guinea, and each one builds its own kind of bower.

1 **The satin** bowerbird makes its bower by stacking twigs in two parallel rows. At the sunny southern end, he makes a dance floor. Then he decorates with colorful objects—navy blue to match his feathers or pale yellow-green to match those of his mate.

2 **When a female** shows an interest, the male dances excitedly and shows off his decorations by holding them in his beak. He may also sing a loud song.

Three styles of bower

The orange-crested gardener's bower resembles an upside-down bowl 3 feet across. A small tree padded with moss anchors it.

The bower of MacGregor's bowerbird resembles a dry Christmas tree ringed by moss and shiny "presents."

Newton's golden bowerbird creates a fence of twigs between two saplings. The male builds up the same bower year after year. He courts the female near his fence.

3 **If she approves** of a male's bower, his treasure, and his dance, the female crouches in the bower, ready to mate.

4 **After mating,** the female flies off to build a nest high in a tree some distance from the bower. She takes full responsibility for incubating the eggs and feeding the young. The male repairs and redecorates his bower in an attempt to attract another female.

Why Do Cranes Dance?

A pair of Japanese cranes on their wintering ground greet each other. With wings outstretched, the birds perform deep knee bends, lower their heads, then stretch up to their full 5-foot height. The cranes may weigh 22 pounds each and may live 50 years.

Courtship rituals in other birds

Many types of birds perform complex courtship rituals, and each type has its own particular ceremony. The birds may dance together, or the male may sing for the female or show off flashy plumage. Sometimes the rituals include a precise series of movements and responses. But no matter what form these performances take, they have an important function. They help the male convince the female that he is not going to attack, and they help to make sure that both partners are of the same species and are ready to mate.

Courting Galapagos albatrosses nibble each other's beaks, stretch, and yawn.

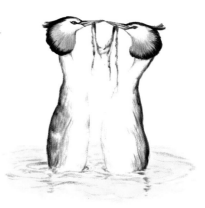

During courtship, crested grebes dive and come up with beaks full of water plants.

Japanese cranes are amazing birds that stand nearly 5 feet tall. In Japan, they are symbols of love and happiness. They mate for life, and couples may dance together year round. The most important dancing, however, is performed during the breeding season, when the cranes dance to express their desire to mate. The male or the female may start a dance by making a high, graceful leap with wings outstretched. The partner slowly circles the leaper. After several leaps, the partners switch dancing roles. Finally the male stands with his wings on display while the female looks on. Once one couple begins, the urge to dance may spread until a whole flock is dancing.

A male crane leaps high into the air to invite his mate to dance. His mate quietly dances a circle around him while he jumps again and again. After some time, the female begins to leap and the male watches. Cranes dance during courtship and also at other times of year—apparently to strengthen the bond between them.

Mated cranes lift their beaks skyward and call together, announcing their territory. The duet may be heard 2 miles away. The female nests on the ground and lays two eggs, but seldom, if ever, raises two chicks.

A female kingfisher begs like a chick. The courting male responds by feeding her a fish.

Male and female jackdaws preen each other's head and neck feathers as they court.

A pair of black-headed gulls stand back to back as part of their courtship ritual.

How Do Male and Female Moles Meet?

Moles spend most of their lives underground in tunnels. Males and females each make their own tunnels and live alone. During the mating season, however, the males and females must find each other. In search of a mate, a male digs new tunnels and explores any that he finds by sniffing the odor left by the owner's scent glands and droppings. He avoids the tunnels of males because a chance meeting may result in a fight. When he finds a female interested in him, they mate. Then the male returns to his own territory and continues his solitary life. In her own home, the female gives birth to about four young after a month-long pregnancy. She nurses the young for only three weeks before they begin to feed on their own.

A mole pokes its head above ground.

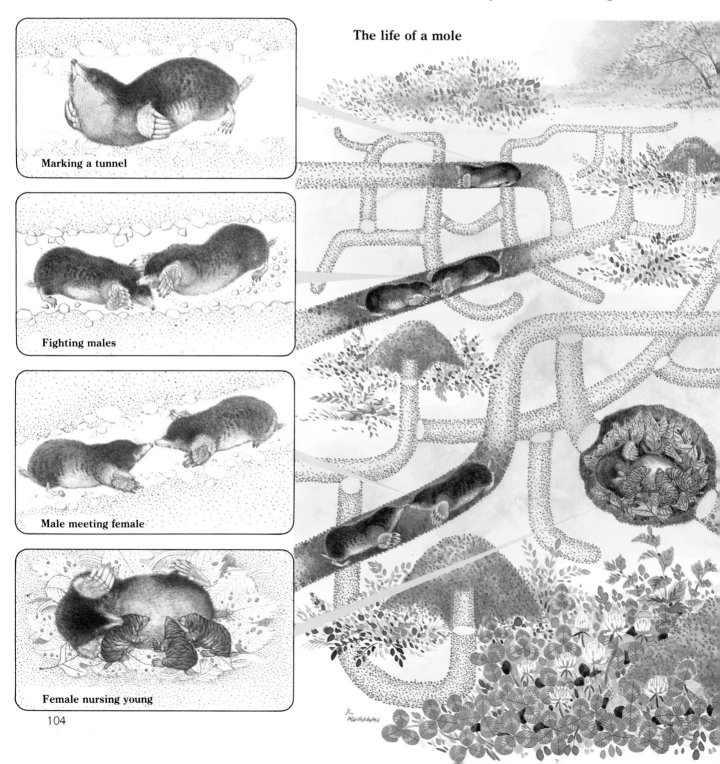

The life of a mole

Marking a tunnel

Fighting males

Male meeting female

Female nursing young

104

A mole's territory

A mole lives in tunnels that form its territory, shown by the black dots at right. Navigating by smell and touch, a mole checks all of its territory every few hours. The tunnels are traps as well as passageways. Earthworms, beetles, and grubs fall into them and are snatched up by the patrolling mole. To keep a steady food supply, moles dig new tunnel sections every day. If a mole finds more food than it can eat, it paralyzes its prey with a bite and stores it in a pantry tunnel to eat later. Moles usually enter each other's territories only during the breeding season.

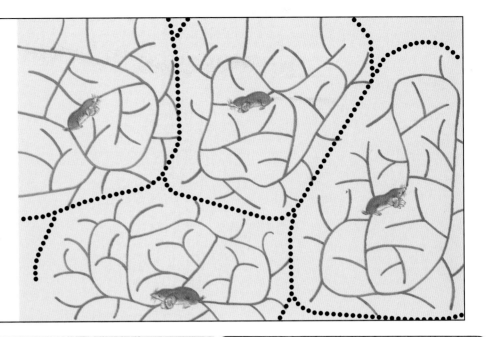

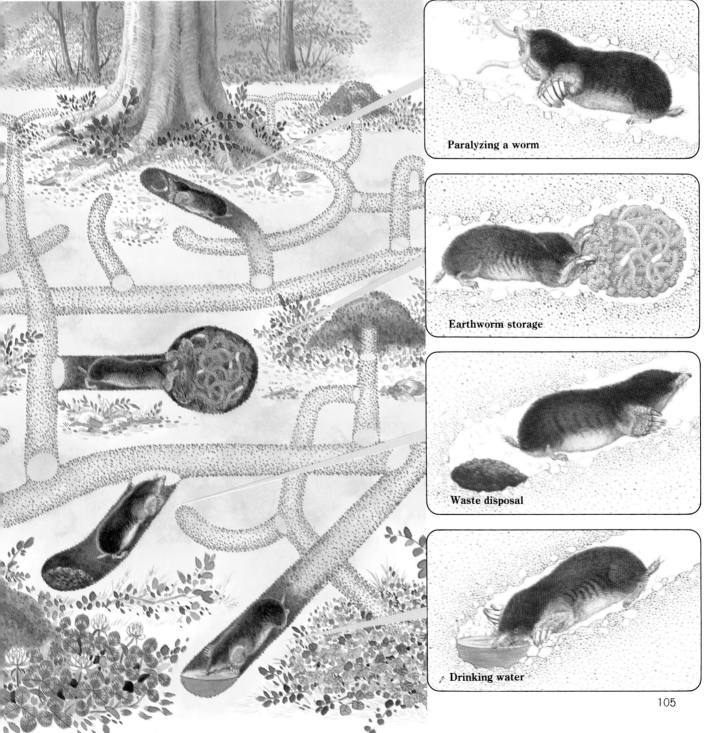

Paralyzing a worm

Earthworm storage

Waste disposal

Drinking water

Why Do Bighorn Sheep Butt Heads?

1 **During the** breeding season, two rams suddenly face off to establish which is the dominant one. They jockey for position, each trying to gain the high ground.

In the fall, bighorn sheep feel the urge to mate. Fights break out, and males, called rams, butt their horned heads together. These head-on fights rarely result in any injury worse than a bloody nose or a broken horn, but sneak attacks from the side often break ribs. The winner, the dominant male, has more opportunities of mating with the females, or ewes, than do the losers. But the losers aren't entirely left out. While the dominant male chases one ram, another ram may mate with his ewe. Or a loser may drive a ewe away from another ram.

2 **As if on cue,** the rival rams rear up on their hind legs. The one standing uphill from the other will be able to gather more speed and hit his opponent harder.

The growth of horns

Rams are capable of mating when they are two years old. But they are only adolescents then and their horns continue to grow. A two-year-old male cannot win a head-on contest with a dominant male, though he may chase a ewe away from him and mate with her. By the time a ram is four years old, his horns have reached a half circle. At six or seven years, the horns are large enough to enable him to challenge older males head on. A ram's horns continue to grow until he reaches eight years of age. His horns would reach a full circle, but in each battle, he loses bits off the tips.

A ram's skull grows along with his horns. The skull is 2 inches thick and has two hard layers with a cushioning layer of frothy bone sandwiched between. A thick layer of hide covers the skull.

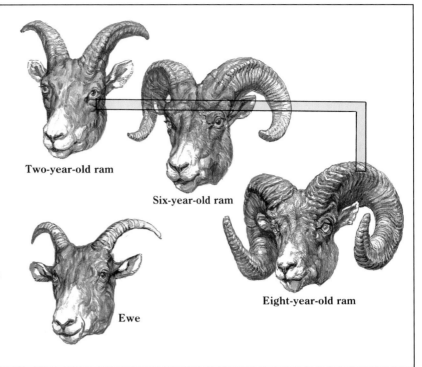

Two-year-old ram

Six-year-old ram

Eight-year-old ram

Ewe

3 **The rams** throw their entire weight at each other; they may weigh as much as 250 pounds. The impact is so great it raises their hind feet off the ground. Afterward, both rams stand quietly, perhaps stunned.

How do rams set up an order of dominance?

Before the breeding season begins, rams live in bachelor herds away from females. They often nuzzle each other, with older, larger males getting the most attention. In October, as the urge to mate increases, the mood changes and young rams begin challenging the dominant rams. A challenger may charge the older, more powerful ram from the rear or the side, rather than chance a frontal attack. If two males are unsure of their place in the order, they will battle head on. The ram that wins most often claims the top of the breeding ladder, taking his choice of females.

Why Do Fiddler Crabs Wave Their Claws?

A female fiddler crab has two small claws that she uses for grasping food. A male fiddler crab has one small claw and one big one. He uses the small claw to eat and the overgrown claw to wave and attract a female during the mating season. If she shows any interest, he waves more frantically, until he can persuade her to scuttle down his burrow in the sand to mate.

In addition to attracting females, a male's large claw warns away other males. Sometimes males fight with these big claws in a sort of seashore wrestling match.

In this species of fiddler crab, the male uses both of his claws to attract the attention of a female. He draws big circles in the air with his huge right claw. At the same time, he bobs the small left claw up and down.

A female fiddler watches the male's display. If she is impressed, she follows him to his burrow to mate.

A male swings his large right claw up and down while lifting his smaller left claw. Finally, he holds both claws overhead.

A male keeps his large left claw level as he waves it up and down in a courtship ritual.

The burrow of a fiddler crab

If a female fiddler follows a male, they mate in his burrow. If a male follows a female, they mate outside her burrow. The burrow contains space for resting and a saltwater supply at the bottom.

A fiddler's burrow may reach 4 feet deep. The crabs dig by packing the sand into little balls that they carry out.

The fiddler's drumroll

In some species of fiddler crab, the males wave their big claws to attract mates when the tide is out during the day. When the tide is out at night, they use sound signals instead. A male taps the surface of the water or the walls of his burrow. A female, sensing the vibrations in the wet sand, looks for their source. She then checks the waving of the claw to make sure the male is of the right species.

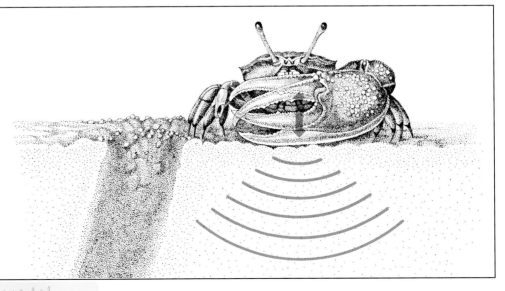

Do Alligators Care for Their Young?

An adult alligator is impressive. It can be 8 to 12 feet long and has jaws that snap powerfully on its prey, most often fish, frogs, and small mammals. But alligators also have a gentle side to them. Unlike most reptiles, female alligators nurture their young to help them survive.

Breeding begins in April, when both sexes bellow loudly and splash their heads noisily into the water to notify other adults that they are ready for mating. When males meet, they fight to establish a dominance order. The most dominant male takes first choice of females and controls the largest territory, but females usually mate with more than one male. After greeting each other by rubbing snouts and coughing gently, a pair mates.

An American alligator breaks free from its eggshell.

The alligator and its young

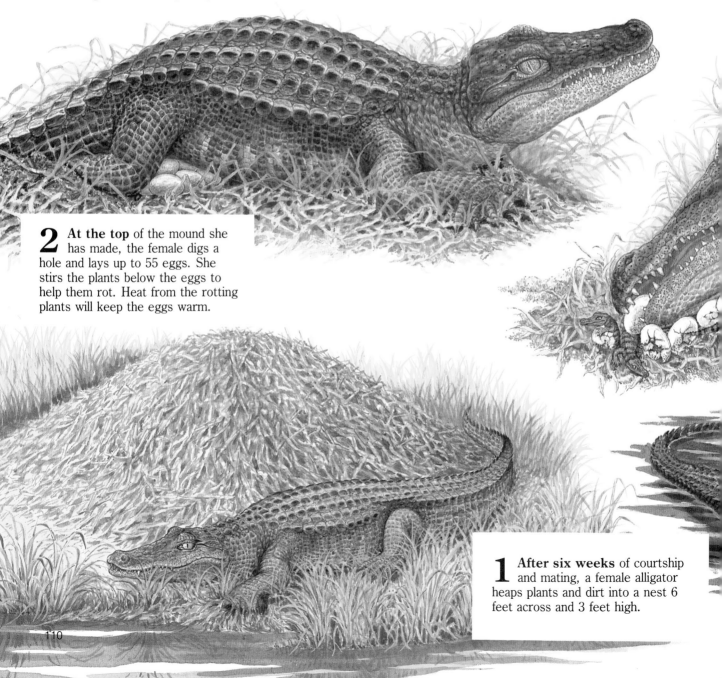

2 **At the top** of the mound she has made, the female digs a hole and lays up to 55 eggs. She stirs the plants below the eggs to help them rot. Heat from the rotting plants will keep the eggs warm.

1 **After six weeks** of courtship and mating, a female alligator heaps plants and dirt into a nest 6 feet across and 3 feet high.

Having used her powerful jaws to ~~pr~~otect her eggs from ~~pr~~edators, the mother ~~no~~w uses them to lift her ~~yo~~ung from the nest.

As they poke through their tough ~~she~~lls, the newborn alli~~gat~~ors squeak. Hearing ~~the~~m, the mother rips ~~ope~~n the nest mound.

5 **The mother** takes some of the young in her mouth, transporting them from the mound to the water. Then she calls for the others to follow along.

6 **The group** of young alligators remains close to the nest. A distress call from them quickly brings a hissing, lunging adult to their defense.

111

How Do Penguins Find Their Chicks?

Penguin parents never enter a crowd of chicks to find their own—they can't tell one chick from another. They stand at the edge of the group instead and squawk loudly. When their chicks hear them, they come running for food.

Newborn chicks depend on their parents for everything. One parent goes for food, while the other sits on the nest, warming the chicks and protecting them from predators. When the absent parent returns with food, it calls to locate its mate among thousands of other penguins, and the parent on the nest responds. By the time the chicks are three weeks old and have joined a crèche—a large group of chicks guarded by just a few adults—they have their parents' voices imprinted in their memory and come when called.

Returning with food, penguin parents call to their young. They give the same call they used to announce their arrival. When the chicks run from the crèche, they are followed by other hungry chicks, but the parents recognize the voices of and feed only their own.

Adélie penguin chicks in the crèche (pronounced kresh) listen to adults calling all around them. When they hear their parents' voices, they run to them and beg for food.

A year in the life of penguins

In late September —early spring in Antarctica—Adélie penguins migrate to their coastal breeding grounds.

Males arrive a week before females to claim nest sites.

A male and a female greet each other before mating.

The female lays two eggs in a sto nest in late Octob

Brown skuas kill and eat penguin chicks that wander away from the safety of the crèche. A lone chick is also exposed to the danger of cold winds.

An adult penguin with no young of its own guards the crèche, driving off an attacking brown skua. Brown skuas, which look like large gulls, nest near penguin colonies and keep a sharp lookout for any unguarded eggs or chicks that they can catch for meals.

An Adélie parent coughs up krill—small shrimplike crustaceans—to feed its chicks.

Eggs hatch in late November; parents keep chicks warm.

Three-week-old chicks gather into a crèche.

In January, newly fledged chicks take to the sea.

113

How Does the Cuckoo Raise Its Young?

Most birds build nests, incubate eggs, and feed their chicks, but not cuckoos. They and a few other species called brood parasites trick other birds into doing all the work for them. A female cuckoo watches another bird's nest until both parents leave. Then she swoops down, snatches up an egg, and lays her own—in about 10 seconds. When the foster parents return, they often accept the new egg and incubate it along with their own. The cuckoo chick usually hatches first and shoves the remaining eggs out of the nest. Then it gets all the food brought by the foster parents for itself.

A female cuckoo scoops an egg from another bird's nest. The nest's owners are off foraging. It takes the cuckoo only a few seconds to lay her egg and leave.

After 11 days, the cuckoo's egg hatches. Before the eggs of the foster parents hatch, the blind cuckoo chick braces its feet and, pushing with its back and wings, rolls the eggs out of the nest.

Cuckoo eggs resemble those of the foster parents

A cuckoo's egg, marked by arrows here, often matches the color and pattern of the other bird's eggs, though it is usually a bit larger. A female cuckoo identifies with its foster parents and will lay in nests of the same species, called its host.

Shrike

Red-tailed shrike

Oriental great reed warbler

Japanese bunting

Azure-winged magpie

↓ Indicates cuckoo's egg

114

A foster parent feeds caterpillars, flies, and bugs to the huge cuckoo chick in its nest, just as it would feed its own young. The fast-growing cuckoo chick will reach a foot in length by the time it is full grown, dwarfing its foster parents.

This two-week-old cuckoo is four times the foster parents' size and has left their nest, but they still feed it. Foster parents sometimes recognize cuckoo eggs and pitch them from their nest. But once the cuckoo has hatched, the foster parents take care of it.

Cuckoos and a new host species

The azure-winged magpies of Japan encountered cuckoos only recently. The magpies lived in the low plains and the cuckoos lived in the grassy highlands. As both species spread, however, their ranges began to overlap. Cuckoos began to lay eggs in magpie nests, and the magpies accepted the new eggs as their own. Now up to 80 percent of magpie nests in some areas may hold cuckoo eggs. In one case, a magpie pair raised five cuckoo chicks, one after the other.

The cuckoo egg *(pink)* is a different color and smaller than the magpie eggs, but the magpies do not reject it.

Having hatched too late to push the magpie's eggs out of the nest, this cuckoo chick *(left)* eats alongside a pair of smaller and less developed magpie chicks.

Do Some Birds Have Help in Rearing Their Young?

Most birds are reared by one or both parents. But some birds have help from other young birds without mates; this is called cooperative breeding.

Only about 300 species of birds cooperate in breeding. The helpers are always the same species as the parents, but not all cooperate in the same way. In some species, the growing chicks may stay and help care for next year's young. Sometimes two or more females share a nest, and sometimes several males mate with a single female.

Cooperative birds include the scrub jays in Florida, the moorhen in Japan, and the Asian stubtail. It may seem the helpers are being generous, but they are really waiting for a nest site, for more abundant food, or for a mate so that they, too, can breed.

Scrub jays share the tasks

Scrub jays in Florida raise families on permanent territories. In about half of the families, one to six chicks remain with their parents, who mate for life. These helpers stay up to six years, protecting and caring for new chicks. Parents with helpers raise more than twice as many chicks as parents alone.

Warblers' co-op

Short-tailed brush warblers spend each summer breeding in the brushy undergrowth of Northeast Asia's woodlands. Only males of this species stay around to help. At first they merely sit on the edge of the nest and chirp. But once the young chicks have grown flight feathers and left the nest, the male parent looks after them. Then the female parent builds a second nest nearby and mates with another male that attended her at the first nest. In this species, unlike scrub jays, some birds benefit immediately by helping—they gain a mate.

Two male helpers watch the female warbler feed her chicks.

A young helper struts toward a snake, trying to scare it away. Because helpers reduce the predators' success, more chicks survive to adulthood.

A helper takes a break from feeding chicks and calls to proclaim the family's territory. Florida's scrub jays thrive only in rare, scattered oak scrub habitat. A helper may have to wait years before finding a territory in which to start its own family.

Cooperative breeding in the moorhen

A species of moorhen that lives in the lakes, marshes, and ponds of Japan also has help in raising its chicks. Each brood of moorhen chicks remains with its parents and helps feed the new chicks. Moorhens hatch three broods a year, and several generations may pass before a moorhen helper leaves its family. The reason why chicks of some species stay around to help is not known for sure. According to one theory, the young stay with their parents because it is hard to become independent. There may be too few females for mating, too little space for territories, or too little food to support larger populations.

A young moorhen feeds its younger sibling.

Why Do Hover Flies Like Aphids?

A female hover fly lays eggs in an aphid colony. In most aphid species, eggs survive the winter and hatch in the spring. Only wingless females emerge from the eggs. These females do not mate and lay eggs. Instead they give birth to new generations of wingless females without being fertilized by males.

Several generations of wingless female aphids may be born on a single plant, quickly creating an enormous population. The aphids are a feast for hover fly larvae. But eventually the aphid population outgrows its home and leaves, which may doom the hover fly larvae.

Hover fly egg laying and aphids

By counting aphids and hover fly eggs, scientists have proved that there is a relationship between the two. In March, the number of aphids in a colony begins to increase. By early April, the population reaches a peak, then levels off. In early May, the population falls. Hover flies lay almost no eggs until about 10 days before the aphid peak and almost none after the peak. By laying only while an aphid colony is growing, hover flies make sure their larvae will have plenty of food. Hover fly females apparently judge the state of aphid populations by the presence or absence of winged female aphids.

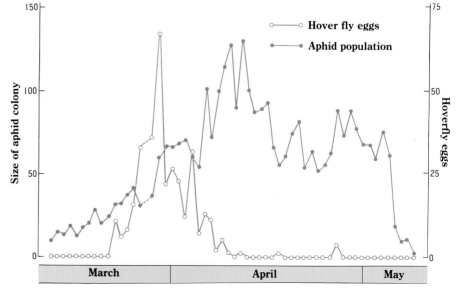

Hover flies look for aphids because female hover flies lay their eggs in colonies of these tiny plant pests. The hover fly eggs hatch into larvae that feed on the aphids until they change into adult flies. But a female hover fly must choose an aphid colony carefully. Aphids are small insects that suck the sap of plants. They can do great damage to plants because they reproduce very fast. Once a colony has become large, aphids develop wings and fly away. Soon the colony dies. To prevent her young from starving, a female hover fly must choose a growing colony rather than one at the peak of its population. If she sees some aphids with wings, a female hover fly ignores that colony and continues looking for a better one in which to lay her eggs.

When the aphid population peaks, females with wings are born. They fly off and form new colonies on fresh plants. Late in the season both males and females with wings are born, and they fly off to mate and lay eggs. The original colony dies out. The hover fly larvae on the plant will probably starve.

Dummy aphids fool the fly

By making fake aphid colonies, scientists learned that it is the wings on aphids that tip the flies off that an aphid colony will not last long. The scientists put groups of different size plastic beads on leaves. They also glued wings on some beads and placed them in groups on other leaves. The different beads represented small, medium, and large aphids. Female hover flies fell for the trick and laid eggs among the fake aphids. But they avoided the groups with the winged beads. The flies seemed to see wings as a signal that a colony is about to disappear.

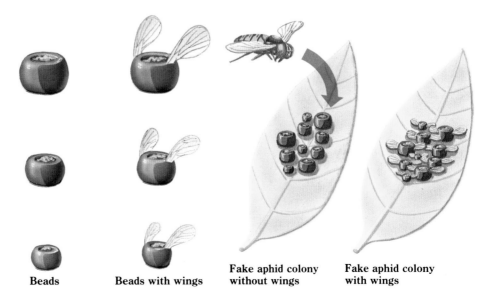

| Beads | Beads with wings | Fake aphid colony without wings | Fake aphid colony with wings |

How Can a Salmon Return to the River of Its Birth?

Salmon are master navigators. Born in rivers, they migrate to the oceans and roam around the world for years. When it is time to breed, they find their way back to the river where they were born. They must navigate the trackless ocean and pass by the mouths of many rivers before finding the one that leads to their birthplace. Exactly how a salmon does this is still a mystery, but researchers think that details about a salmon's birthplace are always in the salmon's memory and that the fish uses three navigational aids—the sun, earth's magnetism, and the salmon's sense of smell—to guide it on its long journey.

Young salmon, or fingerlings, spend the first six months of their lives where they were born, which may be hundreds of miles from the ocean.

Salmon return to their birthplace, mate, lay eggs, and die.

3 A keen sense of smell. As the homebound salmon reach the river they left years ago, a third sense of direction may take over. Researchers think the fish smell the difference between rivers. Rivers smell different because they flow through different kinds of soil and plant life. When the salmon recognize the scent of river water flowing into the ocean, they swim up that river.

Salmon readjust to fresh water before going upriver.

1 **The pull of magnetism.** In deep water or stormy weather, when they cannot see the sun, salmon may use earth's magnetism as a guide. Like compass needles, salmon respond to earth's magnetic fields. When a man-made magnetic field was placed near a group of salmon, they changed their movements to align themselves with it.

2 **A sighting on the sun.** When salmon swim in the shallow water along the coast, they may also use the sun to guide them. Like bees and birds, salmon can keep track of the changing position of the sun throughout the day. This information enters a biological clock that helps them plot their paths with a great degree of accuracy.

Why Do Grunion Lay Their Eggs during a New or Full Moon?

Grunion lay their eggs on the beach along the shores of California and Mexico, breeding from March through September. When the tides are highest—about every 15 days when the moon is either full or new—they rush ashore. Carried by the incoming tide, the grunion are cast onto the sand. Once out of the water, the females dig their tails into the sand and lay their eggs. The males surround the females and deposit their sperm, called milt, which sinks into the sand and fertilizes the eggs *(right)*. Once the mating is complete—it takes only about 30 seconds—the fish catch a wave and return to the ocean.

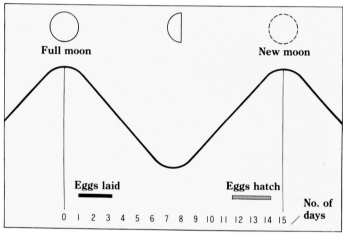

During the breeding season, female grunion lay their eggs on the beach during the two or three nights just after the spring tide. Spring tide occurs when the difference between high and low tide is at its greatest. There is a spring tide whenever there is a full or a new moon.

Why do grunion bury their eggs?

By burying their eggs in the sand, grunion safeguard them from such predators as other types of fish, crabs, and starfish. Later waves may push more sand on top of the eggs. That protects them from birds that probe the sand with their beaks to find food. Female grunion each lay 1,000 to 3,000 eggs in the sand just after the spring tide *(top right)*. As the tides become lower, the eggs remain safely beyond the reach of egg-eating ocean creatures *(center right)*. The next wave to reach the high mark comes after the eggs hatch and carries the young fish to sea *(bottom right)*. It is essential that the grunion lay their eggs shortly after the highest tide, for if they were to lay them when the water is at its highest, the tides would never reach the hatchlings and they would be stranded.

Other spring-tide breeders

Grunion are not the only animals that limit their breeding to the spring tides of the mating season. The globefish and the red-clawed crab, both native to Japan, also spawn during these tides. In its May-to-August breeding season, the globefish lays eggs along rocky coastlines on the five nights before and after each spring tide. The red-clawed crab lives on land, but it spends its larval stage in the ocean. During the breeding season, females gather on the seashore and produce egg masses that develop into larvae. They hold these larvae on their abdomens until the first spring tide. Then they walk into the sea and release the larvae in the water.

Globefish lay eggs among the pebbles along Japan's coast.

Landlubber red-clawed crabs release larvae into the sea.

4
Animal Social Behavior

Many animals live in organized groups, including some species of ants, monkeys, spiders, and birds. Bees build hives, birds form flocks, and mammals from bats to wolves live in groups. In many groups, animals divide the work. This kind of organization is called a social structure. To maintain their structure, social animals communicate among themselves. The languages range from chemical signals passed between insects to gestures and vocal sounds among chimpanzees.

A social structure may be complex. Among ants, for example, workers, soldiers, and the

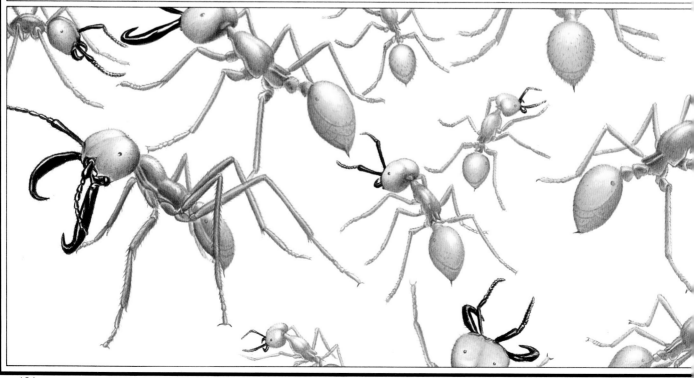

queen all have distinctive shapes that enable them to perform special duties. The role of the queen is to mate and lay eggs. A queen ant that has mated can go off alone to start a new colony with the ants that will hatch from her eggs. When a honeybee colony gets too big, the workers raise a new queen. The queen flies away, and part of the bee colony goes with her in order to build a new home.

One of the simplest social structures consists of one male and his mates, as in a pride of lions. More complicated structures, as among mon- keys and apes, include groups ruled by a hierar- chy of males and others dominated by females. Social structures also vary in size, from a couple that mates for life and their young to groups of hundreds of animals.

Chimpanzees *(above)* form small groups and communi- cate by using sounds and facial expressions. Army ants *(below)* live in colonies of tens of thousands of insects; they use chemicals to send messages to each other.

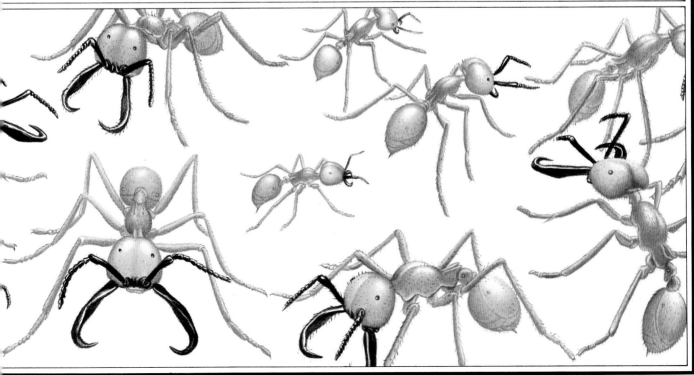

Do Army Ants Really March?

Army ants usually live in large colonies, mainly in the tropics of Africa and South America. The smallest colonies may have 10,000 members, and some in Africa have as many as 30 million. No matter how large the colony, there is only one queen in each; the other ants are workers. Among army ants, many workers also serve as soldiers. The soldiers march in armies to find food—usually insects, including other ants. To keep the supply of food steady, an army ant colony frequently moves its nest to new hunting grounds as much as several hundred yards away.

Army ant settlement

Soldier ant

Queen

Worker ant

Army ants

K. MURAKAMI 90

The traveling phase and the resting phase

A colony of army ants divides its time between traveling and resting. In its traveling phase, the colony moves in a column, camping in a different place each day. During the march, soldiers hunt aggressively to feed the huge numbers of immature ants. In the resting phase, the ants stay in one place for a fixed period. Tropical American army ants travel for 14 to 17 days and rest for 21 days. These times relate to the queen's reproductive cycle. After the first week of rest, the queen's abdomen is swollen with eggs. She lays them by the end of the second week, and soon her abdomen shrinks and she can travel again.

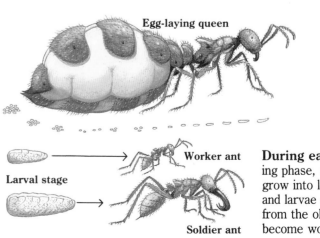

Egg-laying queen

Larval stage

Worker ant

Soldier ant

During each resting phase, eggs grow into larvae, and larvae carried from the old nest become workers.

Soldier ants attacking

orker ants holding legs to form a nest

Old and young workers

n the moving phase, the colony marches n and the new workers join older workers in oraging for food to nourish the new larvae.

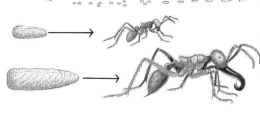

The ants stop for another resting period after two weeks on the march. A chemical secreted by the larvae may trigger the travel and rest cycles.

How Do Bees Keep Busy?

A honeybee is born into one of three distinct castes, or social groups, and does not change to another. Each caste has different duties within the overall social structure of the hive. At the center of each hive is a single queen bee, which lays the eggs. Male drones mate with the queen. Female workers take care of the needs of the hive and all the bees living there.

As the female workers age, they change locations and duties within the hive, gradually moving away from the center. The youngest workers always do the chores that are vital to the hive, such as tending to the young. Older workers build new cells in the honeycombs and repair old ones with wax they exude from their abdomen. There are always more workers than work to be done, so some workers are busy with less important jobs or even remain idle.

1. When workers first emerge from their cells, they clean cells for new eggs. 2. Three-day-old workers nurse the larvae, bringing honey and pollen. 3. One-week-old workers make an orientation flight to learn where the hive is located. 4. At two weeks, workers mend cells, remove waste, or thicken honey. 5. They also guard the entrance, checking the identity of returning workers and cooling the hive by beating their wings. 6. From about the third week, workers collect nectar and pollen as well as resin and water. At night they rest.

Work load of bees

A beehive is constructed so that the cells where larvae are reared are located at the center. Pollen is stored nearby and honey is stored farther out. When new worker bees emerge from the cells at the center, the older bees are slowly forced toward the outer sections of the hive. As they move out, the older workers perform different tasks, depending on the work that is needed where they find themselves. The charts at right show the day-by-day changes in the time that workers devote to different jobs during their short four-week life spans.

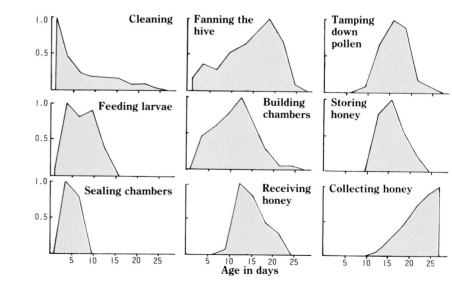

4

5

6

Planing

An activity for idle bees

Because there is sometimes not enough work to go around inside the hive, some workers find themselves with little or nothing to do. They may walk around aimlessly or sit still looking around. Or they may perform the peculiar activity known as planing *(right)*. A worker uses its back and middle legs to push its body back and forth; when it pushes back as far as it can, the worker uses its free forelegs to level off and polish the waxy surface of the honeycomb. The action is called planing because it is similar to the work a carpenter does with a plane to smooth wood.

What Is the Role of Male Bees?

Beekeepers believed for a long time that when a queen bee left her hive on a mating flight all the hive's males, called drones, followed her. Only the strongest of the drones were thought to mate with her. Researchers found this not to be true. In fact, the drones leave the hive every afternoon, whether or not the queen has left. They fly to a specific place where they congregate with drones from other hives. If a queen from any hive arrives there, many of the drones swarming around mate with her.

Every afternoon drones from hives that are near each other mass together in an open area about 50 to 100 yards above the ground. There they buzz around in a huge sphere, usually about 50 yards across. If a large number of drones gathers, the sphere may be as much as 200 yards across.

Castes and shapes of honeybees

Worker (female)

Drone (male)

Queen before mating

Queen heavy with eggs

Drones die after mating. After one drone dies and falls to the ground *(left)*, the queen mates with another. Having mated many times, the queen returns to her hive. She uses the drones' sperm, which is kept in a special sack in her body, to fertilize the eggs that will turn into new bees.

The queen bee flies to the place where the drones congregate. When she arrives, all the drones buzzing about in the area crowd around the queen. She and one of the drones fly together and mate.

Using balloons to find drones

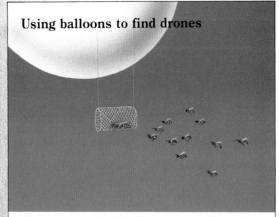

Using helium-filled balloons and radar, scientists study the behavior of drones in the air. The radar measures the size of the sphere of drones. The balloon carries a queen bee in a cage. When the caged queen bee is flown through the drones, the drones in the group detect her pheromones and gather into smaller, tighter groups and pursue her.

Drones in the hive

Drones do not perform any work in the hive. Most of the day they simply wander around, cleaning themselves or getting fed by workers *(above)*. Sometimes drones take honey directly from the cells where it is stored. About a week after becoming adults, drones begin to leave the hive every afternoon for their congregation area. About 30 minutes later they return, are given some honey, and immediately leave again. A drone in good condition repeats this procedure many times. Since a drone dies after mating, the drones that return to the hive have not yet mated.

Why Do Birds Fly in V-Formations?

One reason birds fly in flocks is to make it difficult for predators to pick out a single bird to attack, a strategy that helps small birds. Another reason is to save energy during the birds' long migration flight. This is especially true for large birds, which expend more energy to fly than do smaller birds. When a group of large birds flies in a V-formation, each bird takes advantage of the wind currents generated by the bird that is in front of it. As a bird flies, it creates turbulence in the air. The air directly behind the bird's tail moves downward, while the air behind its wings moves upward. A bird that is following another one puts itself in a position to float on the updrafts that are generated by the leader's wings and thus save energy. When a number of large birds fly together, this positioning automatically results in a V-formation.

Swans fly in V-formation. As they fly, they take turns in the lead position, where flying is hardest.

How small birds fly

In contrast to large birds like swans, whose wings are well suited for flying at an even level, smaller birds, such as sparrows and bulbuls, have wings designed for quick takeoffs and landings. As a result, these birds fly in an up-and-down motion, illustrated below. They alternately flap their wings, which causes them to rise, and then pull their wings to their sides and rest, which causes them to fall.

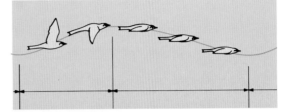

Flocks of bulbuls alternately flutter and glide.

Flying in a V-formation makes efficient use of air currents. As a bird flaps its wings, it creates downdrafts directly behind its tail and updrafts to its sides, behind its wings. By flying to the side of the bird in front, birds get a boost from the updrafts.

How Do Migrating Flocks Navigate?

Using the sun as a guide

A famous experiment with European starlings proved that many birds use the sun as a navigational aid. In the experiment, illustrated at right, starlings were put in a circular cage with six windows through which they could see the sky. On sunny days, the birds faced the direction in which they would normally migrate. Then the researchers installed mirrors at the windows to make the sun look as if it were in a different position. Deceived by the mirrors, the birds faced in the direction they would be migrating if the sun really were in that position. When the sky was overcast and the sun was not visible, the birds did not orient themselves in any particular direction.

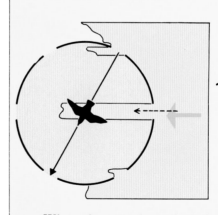

When the sun shone through the eastern window, the starlings turned to the southwest —the direction they would take when migrating.

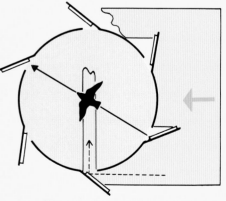

When mirrors changed the apparent direction of the sun by 90 degrees, the birds turned 90 degrees from the proper migratory direction.

Birds that migrate long distances navigate by a variety of methods. When they can see the sun, birds track the sun. Birds have an instinctive knowledge of the sun's movement. No matter where they are, the position of the sun keys birds in to their location and the direction in which they are headed. After the sun sets, birds navigate by the moon and stars. In addition to reading the sun, birds appear to use earth's magnetic fields and gravitational pull to help guide them to their destination.

Migrating over great distances

Of all migratory birds, the Arctic tern travels the farthest. It spends summers above the Arctic Circle, then heads south for summer in Antarctica. Although the terns use a number of different migratory routes *(right),* the most common one spans more than 22,000 miles and runs from Canada past Europe, Africa, and South America to Antarctica. By migrating over such vast distances, Arctic terns enjoy summer year-round. Like other birds, they navigate by observing the position of the sun and by a still unknown way of detecting and interpreting earth's magnetic fields and, perhaps, gravity.

Migratory routes of Arctic terns

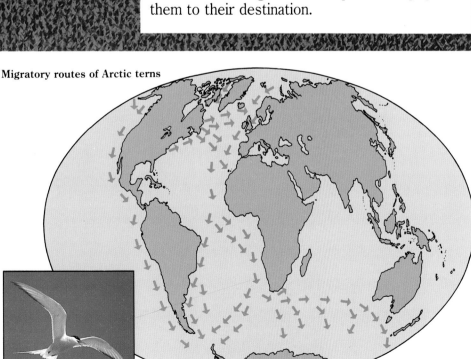

Arctic tern

How Can Birds Fly at Night without Seeing Landmarks?

▲ Flycatcher

Birds navigate by the stars

In experiments done in the 1960s and 1990s, researchers placed birds in a planetarium and projected an image of the night sky onto the planetarium's dome. When the stars were bright, the birds flew in the direction they normally take when migrating *(bottom left)*. However, when the researchers turned off the projection of the stars, the birds flew in all directions *(bottom right)*. They were confused by the lack of any orienting stars.

Flight patterns with stars *(left)*
and without stars *(right)*

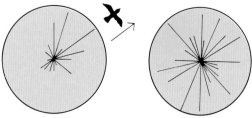

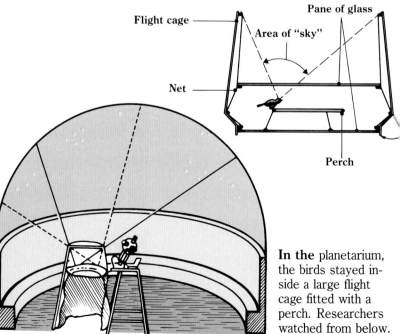

In the planetarium, the birds stayed inside a large flight cage fitted with a perch. Researchers watched from below.

Birds that migrate long distances fly at night as well as during the day. Some small land birds fly nonstop for 86 hours to cross 2,300 miles of ocean. How do they find their way at night, when they cannot see the landmarks and the position of the sun that guide them during the day? They note the positions of the moon and stars. And when the sky is clouded over and the moon and stars are not visible, birds may get a fix on their position by aligning themselves with earth's magnetic field.

Sensing earth's magnetic field

Birds appear to have a magnetic compass in their brains that orients them with earth's magnetic field. In an experiment, researchers attached small magnets to the necks of pigeons. When released to fly to their nest, the birds had no problem navigating on sunny days, but experienced difficulties on overcast days. This suggests that the birds navigated well on sunny days because they used the sun to orient themselves and that they navigated poorly on cloudy days because the magnets interfered with their reading of earth's magnetism. When the magnets were replaced with lead weights, the pigeons navigated well on both sunny and cloudy days. They apparently could use earth's magnetism as a guide.

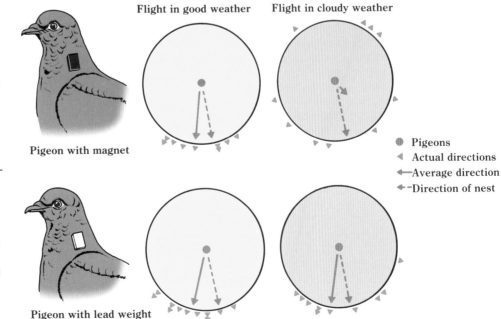

Flight in good weather

Flight in cloudy weather

Pigeon with magnet

Pigeon with lead weight

● Pigeons
◀ Actual directions
←Average direction
←-Direction of nest

How Do Lions Live Together?

Lions are social animals and live in family groups called prides. A pride has up to a dozen adult females, one to six adult males, and several cubs. Female cubs stay with the pride when they grow to maturity, but young adult males are chased away by the pride's dominant male.

Females hunt to provide food for the pride. They hunt as a group, often sneaking into positions around a zebra or other prey so that it cannot escape. The lionesses share their kills with the males and cubs.

Although they are much larger than females, male lions hunt only when they do not belong to a pride. Males in a pride reserve their fighting for combat with other lions. When a strange male enters the pride's territory, the dominant male tries to drive it away by a show of strength. If that fails, they fight. Young males that have left the pride wander around in groups until they can take over a pride of their own and mate.

Male members of a pride do not fight each other, but when an outsider tries to take over a territory or a pride, the battle is fierce. The loser sometimes dies. For this reason, males often avoid fights, with the smaller lion backing down. A lion's mane may make him look bigger and thus make other males avoid fighting him.

Changes within a pride of lions

The group of females in a pride changes only with births or deaths, but male leaders may come and go through competition with other males. When a new male wins the leadership of the pride, he may kill some of the cubs born of his predecessor. Soon afterward, the mothers of those cubs mate with the new leader. Ordinarily, a female lion raises her cubs until they are about two years old, and during that time she does not mate again. By killing the cubs, the new leader ensures that he does not have to wait two years before he can mate and produce his own cubs. This increases the chance that his offspring will be more numerous and that some will survive even if he is soon driven off by other males taking over the pride.

The female cubs stay with the pride, but the males leave or are chased off by the leader.

A stable pride has a leader, several females, and their cubs.

Some cubs are killed by the new leader. Their mothers mate with the leader to have new cubs.

A female watches over the pride's cubs. All the pride's females cooperate in raising the young. Mothers nurse any cub, without distinguishing between their own offspring and those of other females in the pride.

A male that has just taken over a pride from another male may kill some of the cubs sired by the previous leader. But in general males ignore cubs and they do not kill their own.

A lone male is interested in a pride and approaches it to see if he has a chance to take over and mate with the females.

The pride leader and the outsider do battle over the pride.

The leader dies trying to defend his rights, and the victor takes over the pride.

What Are Primates' Social Groups?

Primates—monkeys and apes—almost always live in groups. Among the nearly 200 different species of primates, however, social structures vary widely. In some, males and females meet only during the mating season; in others, they mate for life. Males and females may have a single mate, or they may mate with several members of the group. For example, female tamarin monkeys of South America have several mates. They usually give birth to two young at a time and then the males raise the youngsters. In another type of primate society, hamadryas baboons live in harems made up of one mature male and several females. Several harems combine to form a band, and bands meet to form sleeping troops of as many as 750 baboons.

A monogamous relationship

Gibbons are monogamous, which means they have only one mate and stay with this mate for life.

Independent existence

Orangutans are among the few primates that do not form groups. They mate only in the breeding season, when a male visits several females. The young live with their mothers until they are mature enough to leave.

A matriarchal society

Macaques live in large clans that include males, females, and their offspring. When young males mature, they leave to join another clan or live alone. Females, who stay with the clan, form a hierarchy based on who their parents were, with the high-ranking females dominating.

● **A patriarchal society**

A chimpanzee clan centers on several males that live in groups and defend a territory that includes the ranges of several females. Females and the young live apart most of the time but gather around a good source of food.

Do Chimpanzees Use Language?

The vocal organs of chimpanzees cannot produce speech, and their hearing, while sharp, does not allow them to distinguish the sounds in complex spoken language. However, chimpanzees do communicate a variety of messages by glances, by expressions *(below),* and by postures and an assortment of calls and vocal noises. The sounds a chimpanzee makes include groans, cries, screams, and noises that sound like gasping or panting. The wide range of expressive techniques that chimpanzees use could well be described as a language.

Facial language

A scowl indicates that a chimpanzee is about to threaten or attack an adversary. The chimp makes no sound, but the hair on its head stands on end.

This expression accompanied by several hoots, occurs when a chimp discovers plentiful food or meets other chimpanzees.

Roars replace hoots when a chimpanzee communicates with distant clan members. A roar can be heard a half mile away.

A subordinate chimp bares its teeth when it is startled, afraid, or approaching a dominant individual.

An open-mouthed smile, accompanied by gasps, may express either surprise when caught unawares or an invitation to play.

A gaping mouth and a scream indicate great excitement or surprise.

To admit defeat, a chimpanzee mimics an infant chimp's pouting appeal to its mother.

142

Body language

Besides calls and facial expressions, the ways the body, hands, and arms are used are important in chimpanzee communication. Observers have found a wealth of meaning in gestures and postures, and some of these are shown below and at right. Like human beings, chimpanzees kiss and hug, clap their hands, and greet each other when meeting after a separation. Communication is necessary for maintaining their social order.

Greeting its superior, a small chimpanzee extends its hands as it bends low to the ground in a bow.

A chimp shows it wants some of a companion's food by gazing intently and holding out a hand.

A shaking, outstretched arm repels an intruder.

Kisses are used to greet relatives and close friends. Chimp parents often exchange kisses with their offspring, which strengthens their bond.

A male drags a branch around to intimidate a clan member or an enemy.

Talking with apes

When chimpanzees and gorillas are taught sign language or the meaning of symbols, they remember the meanings and the word order. By using a special keyboard with the symbols shown at right, trained chimps can carry on simple but meaningful conversations with humans, forming correct sentences to express their wish for food, drink, and play.

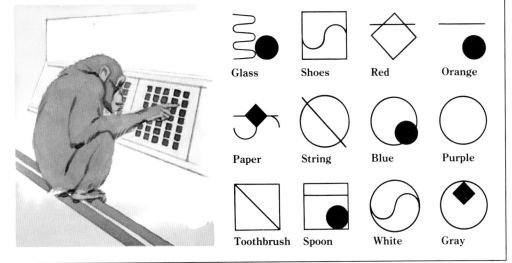

Glass	Shoes	Red	Orange
Paper	String	Blue	Purple
Toothbrush	Spoon	White	Gray

Can Monkeys Learn from Each Other?

One monkey may discover a new activity and teach it to its young; finally, the whole social group may copy it. For example, a two-year-old Japanese macaque named Imo accidentally discovered that washing her sweet potatoes before eating them removed gritty dirt. Later, her whole group began washing potatoes. Shortly after that the monkeys started soaking sweet potatoes in seawater to give them a salty taste, a unique practice that has become firmly established as part of the group's habits.

A **Japanese macaque** cleans sandy grain by washing it in a puddle. The sand sinks and the clean grain floats. Once the monkey figured this out, others copied it.

In a cold, mountainous region of Japan, monkeys keep warm in a hot spring. After one monkey discovered the warmth by jumping in, others followed its example.

Glossary

Adaptation: An inherited change in structure, function, or form that improves an animal's or a plant's chance of reproducing and surviving in its environment.

Amino acid: A chemical compound that forms structural units of proteins.

Antenna: One of a pair of jointed, movable feelers, or sensory receptors, on the front of an animal's head, as in insects, spiders, or crustaceans.

Anus: The opening at the end of the digestive tract through which undigested materials are eliminated from the body.

Apes: Large primates, including chimpanzees and gorillas.

Baleen: Sievelike plates in the mouths of certain types of whales that have no teeth; the plates are used for straining food from the water.

Barbels: Slender feelers, containing taste buds, that grow from the lips or jaws of certain fish, including catfish and loach.

Camouflage: Protective adaptation that allows an animal to blend into its environment, reducing its chance of being detected.

Carapace: A hard protective shell covering the back of some animals, such as crabs and turtles.

Carbon dioxide: A gas made up of molecules consisting of one carbon atom and two oxygen atoms; a by-product of respiration in animals that is used by plants during photosynthesis to produce oxygen and other compounds.

Cartilage: Flexible connective bone tissue that gives support and allows some movement.

Caste: A specialized form of an insect that lives in a colony, such as worker bees among honeybees. Each caste carries out its own particular job in the colony.

Chromatophores: A pigment-bearing cell in some animals that allows them to change color.

Cilia: Short, hairlike structures on the surface of certain single-celled animals, such as the paramecium. Cilia are used for movement and to pull in food.

Dermis: A layer of skin underneath the epidermis, made of elastic connective tissue that supports and binds the skin to muscle and bone.

Echolocation: The process of finding an object by using sound waves, which are reflected off the object to the sender; the process bats use to find food.

Enzyme: A protein that affects biochemical reactions.

Epidermis: The outer layer of skin that protects the dermis.

Epithelial cells: Cells that cover body surfaces, form glands, and line body cavities and organs.

Fingerling: A fish under one year of age.

Gall: A tumorlike swelling of plant tissue usually caused by fungi or insects.

Gland: A specialized group of cells that produce and secrete a substance used by the organism.

Grub: Insect larvae—mostly beetles—that are usually found in the ground.

Heredity: The transmission of characteristics from one generation to another.

Hierarchy: A system in which a group of animals, such as chimpanzees, are organized into ranks, with the lower-ranked members subordinate to the more dominant ones.

Hormones: Compounds that are produced by glands and carried by the bloodstream to another organ or tissue where they regulate body functions.

Hyoid bone: A bone that supports the tongue and is located at its base. The hyoid is elongated in woodpeckers.

Instinct: An inborn tendency to behave in a certain way.

Jacobson's organ: A scent organ located in the mouth of some reptiles, as in snakes.

Larva: An immature, wormlike form that hatches from the eggs of many insects and crustaceans.

Macronucleus: The larger nucleus in protozoa, as in the paramecium, that have two nuclei; the other smaller nucleus is called the micronucleus.

Mandibles: Jaws.

Matriarchal society: A society that is ruled by the females of the species.

Melanophores: Black or brown pigment-bearing cells.

Membrane: A thin layer of tissue often covering or lining an organ.

Migration: The periodic move made by some animals between winter feeding grounds and summer breeding grounds.

Mimicry: A type of adapted camouflage in which one species resembles another or a species takes on the appearance of an object of its environment, such as a twig or a flower petal. **Batesian mimicry** is the resemblance of a harmless species to a dangerous or vile-tasting one. **Müllerian mimicry** means different species of poisonous animals resemble each other.

Molting: Periodic shedding of skin, fur, feathers, shell, or horn.

Olfactory organ: An organ that receives odors and transmits the sense of smell.

Organ: A body part, such as the heart or the stomach, that performs specific functions.

Pedipalps: The second pair of legs, located just behind the fangs, in spiders.

Perichondrium: The membrane that covers cartilage, except in joints.

Pheromone: A chemical substance secreted by certain animals, such as moths, to signal their location to prospective mates.

Pit organs: Heat-sensing organs located in two hollows below the eyes of snakes.

Pituitary gland: A gland located in the brain that produces hormones influencing body growth.

Predators: Animals that kill and eat other animals.

Primates: An order of animals, including humans, apes, and monkeys, with grasping hands and flexible feet.

Proboscis: In mammals, a long flexible snout or trunk; a tubular organ used for gathering food.

Regeneration: Regrowth of lost body parts, such as tails on lizards and claws on crabs.

Species: A group of organisms that are similar and can breed only among themselves. Part of the classification system *(right)*.

Spinnerets: Silk-spinning organs, as in spiders and caterpillars.

Symbiosis: The close association between two different types of organisms to the benefit of one or both of them. In **mutualism**, both organisms benefit from the relationship; in **commensalism**, one benefits, but the other is not affected; in **parasitism**, one organism benefits at the expense of the other, which is called the **host**.

Taxis: Movement of a simple animal, such as a paramecium, in response to a stimulus. Movement toward a stimulant is known as positive taxis; movement away is known as negative taxis.

Territory: An area that is defended by an individual or a group against intrusions by other members of the species; an animal will hunt for food, court a mate, and raise a family in its territory.

Trichocyst: Barbed projectile in simple animals, such as the didinium, used for defense or capturing food.

Trifurcated nerve: Nerve with three branches that links sensory organs.

Tympanic membrane: Eardrum.

Vacuole: Fluid-filled cavity in simple animals; food is digested in food vacuoles.

Classification of animals

Scientists have recorded some 800,000 different species of animals, but there may actually be twice as many. To handle this great diversity, scientists developed an orderly classification system that groups animals together by their natural relationships. Within the animal kingdom, there are nine major groups called phyla: the sponges, cnidaria, flatworms, roundworms, annelids, mollusks, arthropods, echinoderms, and chordates. Each phylum is divided into classes; each class in turn is subdivided into orders; and each is further grouped in ever more specific classifications, as in the example below. Some animals from the phylum arthropods, for example, are crabs, shrimp, spiders, and mosquitoes. The phylum chordates includes humans, wolves, frogs, sharks, and snakes.

Kingdom:	Animal
Phylum:	Chordate
Class:	Mammal
Order:	Carnivore
Family:	Canidae
Genus:	Canis
Species:	Canis lupus
Common name:	Gray wolf

Index

Staff for
UNDERSTANDING SCIENCE & NATURE

Editorial Directors: Patricia Daniels, Karin Kinney
Writer: Mark Galan
Assistant Editor/Research: Elizabeth Thompson
Editorial Assistant: Louisa Potter
Production Manager: Prudence G. Harris
Senior Copy Coordinator: Jill Lai Miller
Production: Celia Beattie
Library: Louise D. Forstall
Computer Composition: Deborah G. Tait (Manager), Monika D. Thayer, Janet Barnes Syring, Lillian Daniels

Special Contributors, Text: Margery duMond, Stephen Hart, Pat Holland, Fran Moshos, Peter Pocock, Howard Robinson, Brooke C. Stoddard
Design/Illustration: Antonio Alcalá, Caroline Brock, Justine Fasciano, Nicholas Fasciano, Yin Yi
Research: Pat Holland
Index: Barbara L. Klein

Consultants:
J. Thomas Bell, DVM, is an academic dean of the College of Veterinary Medicine, Mississippi State University.
Ronald Crombie of the Smithsonian Institution is an expert on reptiles and amphibians.
Carol Sheppard and Steven Sheppard are entomologists with the U.S. Department of Agriculture.
George Watson of St. Albans School, Washington, D.C., is an ornithologist.

Library of Congress Cataloging-in-Publication Data
Animal behavior.
      p.   cm. — (Understanding science & nature)
     Includes index.
     Summary: Presents in question and answer format information about the behavior of a wide variety of creatures, ranging from the paramecium to the chimpanzee.
     ISBN 0-8094-9658-5 (trade). — ISBN 0-8094-9659-3 (lib. bdg.)
     1. Animal behavior—Miscellanea—Juvenile literature.
[1. Animals—Miscellanea.   2. Questions and answers.]
I. Time-Life Books. II. Series.
QL751.5.A55   1991
591.51—dc20   91-30286
                                    CIP
                                    AC

TIME-LIFE for CHILDREN ™

Publisher: Robert H. Smith
Managing Editor: Neil Kagan
Editorial Directors: Jean Burke Crawford, Patricia Daniels, Allan Fallow, Karin Kinney, Sara Mark
Editorial Coordinator: Elizabeth Ward
Director of Marketing: Margaret Mooney
Product Manager: Cassandra Ford
Assistant Product Manager: Shelley L. Shimkus
Business Manager: Lisa Peterson
Assistant Business Manager: Patricia Vanderslice
Administrative Assistant: Rebecca C. Christoffersen
Special Contributor: Jacqueline A. Ball

Original English translation by International Editorial Services Inc./ C. E. Berry

First printing. Printed in U.S.A.
Published simultaneously in Canada.
Time Life Inc. is a wholly owned subsidiary of
THE TIME INC. BOOK COMPANY.
TIME-LIFE is a trademark of Time Warner Inc. U.S.A.
For subscription information, call 1-800-621-7026.